Maybe I'm NOT Listening

Confessions of a Shrink

Gerald Tarlow, Ph.D.

iUniverse, Inc.
New York Bloomington

Maybe I'm Not Listening
Confessions of a Shrink

iUniverse books may be ordered through booksellers or by contacting:

iUniverse
1663 Liberty Drive
Bloomington, IN 47403
www.iuniverse.com
1-800-Authors (1-800-288-4677)

ISBN: 978-0-595-48303-7 (pbk)
ISBN: 978-0-595-60391-6 (ebk)

Printed in the United States of America

To Michael:

May your chosen profession give you a sense of
fulfillment, happiness and many laughs.

Acknowledgements

In the acknowledgment sections of many books written by psychologists there is often thanks given to professors and other colleagues who had a great influence on their careers. My main goal in writing this book is not to educate, but entertain. If I have done a good job then there are certain people who should be acknowledged for their support of my writing and sense of humor. Most of my English professors would not be included in this list since few of them thought I was a native of the English language. Comedians such as George Carlin and Robin Williams who can make you laugh at some of the very strange things that actually happen in the world are true inspirations. I would like to thank all my friends who actually laughed at my stories and jokes from the time I was a kid till now. Thanks to everyone who appreciated the Tarlow News and looked forward to it arriving every year. Thanks to my family for allowing me to joke with them, sometimes too often. Thanks to my son Michael for appreciating humor at such an early age and trying to make others laugh. And finally, thanks to my wife Nan for laughing and smiling and playing the straight man for over 25 years.

Introduction

I am a clinical psychologist, a psychotherapist, who some call a shrink, a head shrinker, a therapist or a counselor. I have probably been called many other things by some of my patients that they have not shared with me. I started seeing patients in graduate school in 1971, which means I have been practicing for well over thirty years. I know it is an old joke, but I am sure I will be done practicing and be able to be a real therapist very soon. I have been licensed to practice psychology in California since 1978 and have been in full time private practice since 1986. I generally see twenty to twenty-five individual patients every week and direct an intensive program for obsessive-compulsive disorder at UCLA. The UCLA position occupies about six hours per week. It may not seem to you that twenty-five hours plus six hours equals full time work, but it is. I have often wanted to add up all the time I spend per week on the phone. Talking to potential patients, talking to current patients, talking to past patients, talking to psychiatrists and other therapists of past, current, or potential patients, talking to insurance companies, talking to UCLA staff, talking to UCLA students, talking to reporters and talking to building management when I need a light bulb replaced.

I consider myself a specialist. I primarily treat people with anxiety disorders. The most common problems I treat are phobias, panic attacks and obsessive-compulsive disorder. These problems make up about ninety percent of my practice.

The type of therapy I do is called cognitive behavioral therapy. It is a very directive type of therapy that involves teaching people skills and giving them assignments to help them overcome their problems. I think I am very good at this but it took me many years to realize it.

There is no national ranking of therapists, although there are times I wish there were. I think it would motivate me to try to get into the top ten. I would even try to figure out ways of making any of the therapists above me on the list look bad. "Hey, did you hear about Dr. Topdog? I heard three of his patients had to be hospitalized." I am a very competitive person.

I did achieve one measure of status and competence a few years ago. I became a Diplomate in Behavior Therapy from the American Board of Professional Psychology. This was an achievement in which you have to do more than just pay $300 and receive a plaque. It is the most prestigious advanced recognition a practicing psychologist can receive. There are actually less than seventy psychologists in the U.S. who are Diplomates in Behavior Therapy. And, it allows me to put four more initials after my name: ABPP. Granted, none of my patients, and even most other therapists, have any idea what the initials stand for.

Psychologists have written many books. Some books are written for other professionals in order to help them learn techniques of psychotherapy. Some are "self-help" books that are written for people with specific problems. Some are books that analyze the patients the psychologist is seeing. However, there have been very few books that actually tell you what the therapist is thinking. I think this book is unique. I want to give you a real idea of what goes through one therapist's head. Not just about the problems patients are having, but what the therapist is really thinking and, most of time, is unable to say to the patient. I can already picture some of the reviews of this book by "colleagues." "Dr. Tarlow is a burnt out psychologist who doesn't represent the majority of therapists in practice." They may be right. I may be burnt out from seeing so many patients for so many years. I can't claim that all therapists have similar thoughts about their patients and their work. However, I certainly have many friends who are psychotherapists who do share many of the same thoughts.

All of the patients presented in this book are actual patients. Their identities have been changed considerably to try to prevent them from suing me. None of them have given me permission to use their names. None of them knew I would be writing about them. I can't imagine asking a patient, "Do you mind my writing a little about how crazy you are?" I have altered many details about their cases to insure their confidentiality. Given the nature of many of my confessions, I may not have many patients once this book is published.

CHAPTER 1
October

October 1

I have six patients scheduled for today. My first patient is scheduled at ten a.m. Let's call her BK. BK left me a message at nine forty-eight p.m. the previous night telling me she had been meaning to call me for a few days to let me know that she couldn't make the Tuesday appointment. However, she forgot to call and was now informing me that she had an important business meeting to attend. She also said that she understood if I had to charge her for the time since she did not give me twenty-four hours advance notice. I'm sure you want to know if I will charge her. Absolutely. Confession number one: Even though I am not a religious man, after being in private practice forever I sometimes pray for these short notice cancellations. I get to be paid for having a leisurely lunch and reading Newsweek. BK has bragged to me that her billing rate is $250 to $400 per hour for the work she does. Let's do the math. She goes to her business meeting and earns $300 and then has to pay me $200. Ka-ching! She makes $100 even if she pays me. I might have a little more empathy if BK hadn't canceled or if she hadn't missed about twenty sessions over the past year.

Generally, I have anywhere from four to eight patients scheduled in a day. I try to never have more than five patients in a row scheduled without a one-hour break. I think my record was eleven patients in a row without a break. It was a day in which I planned on a few cancellations and everyone showed up. Each session is forty-five minutes. Therapy sessions used to be fifty minutes. Most therapists want to leave the ten or fifteen minutes between patients to "recover" and prepare themselves for the next patient. However, some therapists have reasoned that if they do forty-five minute sessions they can see two patients back to back in one and a half hours. Now, I originally thought this was a good idea. However, trying to get a patient to leave at exactly the end of the session is easier said than done. Many patients have this habit of saving the most important things to say for the last five minutes. "Hey, Doc: I know I only have a few minutes left today, but I wanted to tell you that I had thoughts of killing myself last night." I am now stuck with trying to figure out a solution to his problem in two minutes.

You may want to know how a therapist gets a patient out of his office if the patient does not want to leave. I do tell patients that their time is up. I tell them the next patient is already waiting. If that doesn't work I try getting up and opening the door. There are times I have felt like calling AAA to tow them out of my office. "Yes, AAA I have a 1971 neurotic that is stuck. How soon can you get here?"

I hardly ever see two patients in a row without a fifteen-minute break. I use the break to return phone calls, write notes, go to the bathroom, and talk to people without psychological problems. Unfortunately, there are times when the only people to talk to are other therapists in my suite, and I am not so sure that they don't have psychological problems.

I look forward to finishing on Tuesdays because I generally have Wednesdays off. Confession number two: I never tell patients that I don't work on Wednesdays. When they ask if I have any openings on Wednesday I just tell them that I am booked. I wouldn't want them thinking that I wouldn't make room for them.

October 3

On Thursdays I practice in Calabasas. The office is about five minutes from home so I don't spend any time on the freeway. Therefore, I am always in a great mood to see patients in Calabasas.

Also, I only schedule patients from eight a.m. to three p.m., so I know I have the afternoon and evening to play.

At one p.m. I see OP. OP is a thirty-three year-old, single Caucasian male who I have seen longer than any other patient. I started seeing him fifteen years ago. No, it is not Woody Allen. What is very strange about this is the fact that I inform all new patients that the type of therapy I do is short term. Generally I see patients for three to six months on a once-a- week basis. Occasionally I will have a patient who I see for a year or two, but not fifteen years. So, you may want to know a little about this patient and his problems in order to understand this extended treatment. This patient has a very severe case of obsessive-compulsive disorder (OCD). Obsessions are intrusive, repetitive thoughts and compulsions are ritualistic or repetitive behaviors. (If you still not sure what OCD is, try watching an episode of "Monk.") I would like to share with you one of OP's obsessions. He is afraid he will turn black, as in become an African-American. This has led him to avoid looking at African American people or saying the letters "O.J." I have treated hundreds of OCD patients and, I have to assure you, this is the only patient that I have ever heard of with this obsession. Confession number three: There are times when patients reveal to you a very strange problem it is necessary to look concerned on the outside while laughing hard on the inside. This is a skill that is not taught in graduate school, but can be mastered over time.

You might want to know what a psychologist does with a patient who has this type of obsession. Well, the treatment of choice for OCD is called exposure and response prevention. That means actually exposing the patient to what they fear and not allowing the patient to engage in any compulsive behaviors. Let's face it; it is very difficult to actually make this patient's skin black. So what I did was to take a digital picture of him and change his skin color to black. This worked fairly well for this patient. Why then am I still seeing this patient after fifteen years? Unfortunately, he has many other OCD symptoms that he refuses to address. So, he comes in each week and tells me when he will be ready to address the next symptom. I have tried to tell him many times that I don't have anything new to offer him. However, he continues to want to see me. Most therapists would never complain about this type of behavior. In fact, they would want an entire practice of patients who would never quit therapy. I often wonder what I will tell OP when I retire.

October 4

I have five patients scheduled today. At three p.m. I see RC. RC is afraid of elevators. You need to know that my office is on the eleventh floor. I have always had offices on high floors of office buildings to be able to take advantage of some great views in L.A. Through the years I have "lost" about a dozen patients who have refused to come to my office because it was on an upper floor. However, if the patient is just afraid of elevators, and not heights, they often will climb the stairs to see me. Treating a patient with an elevator phobia is easy. First you teach the patient how to physically relax and breathe. Then you have to help the patient change some very distorted thoughts about elevators and what could happen in an elevator. Here are some examples. "I will be stuck in the elevator and run out of air." "The elevator will break down and no one will know I am in there and I will die." "The elevator will get stuck for a long time and I will have to go the bathroom." "I will starve to death." The irrationality of some of these thoughts never ceases to amaze me. Yet I empathically help the patient to change these thoughts. Confession number four: Sometimes I just want to shout, "Do you know how ridiculous that is! That has never happened to anyone in the history of the world!" So far I have been able to restrain myself.

Treatment for RC today involves spending the full session with him riding up and down the elevator. This is a very interesting way of earning a living. There is an important principle in psychology called habituation. Essentially it means stay in the feared situation long enough and your anxiety will go away. So, my major task with RC is to convince him to stay in the elevator for the full session. Generally this is no problem, today being no exception. However, this treatment does occasionally tap into one of my mild fears: social anxiety. Confession number five: I often wonder what some people are thinking of me when they see me on the elevator several times in a short period. My anxiety seems to rise when the security guards in the building flash me a very quizzical look. I don't think I look like a terrorist, but who can tell these days. As usual RC is quite successful within this session. He is much less anxious than when he started, and he has now spent more time in an elevator today than the last ten years combined.

October 5

I am licensed as a psychologist in California by the Board of Psychology. In its infinite wisdom the Board has decided that psychologists need thirty-six hours of "continuing education" every two years in order to renew the license. Continuing education sounds like something very valuable in principle. In reality, it is a farce. You can't force someone to learn. People need to be motivated on their own to improve their skills and learn about new laws and procedures. The best psychologists I know read journals frequently. No, you don't get continuing education for reading journals or books. You get continuing education credit by attending lectures and workshops that have been approved by specific governing organizations. I hate working on weekends and rarely ever schedule any patients on weekends. However, to fulfill my continuing education requirements I generally have to attend these lectures on weekends. How does one go about choosing which course to take? The first criterion is: How far away from my home is the class? No way will I travel two hours each way to see someone interesting. The second criterion is cost. I refuse to spend $200 to hear a boring speaker. After choosing my classes carefully, I have to prepare for the day. I pack my electronic organizer, games included, and the most recent issues of Sports Illustrated and Newsweek and I am set for the day. The bigger the lecture the easier it is to just sit in back and read or play games. I can even write this book during the lecture. I try to be discreet. I put the organizer in my lap or somewhere hidden amongst some papers. However, there are a few people who have no social anxiety and are blatantly flaunting their disinterest. One person is reading the LA Times. He holds the paper up in front of him while the lecturer is speaking. I have seen other people put their head down and fall asleep. You can't force people to learn!

When the continuing education requirements were first put in place psychologists were required to sign in at the beginning of the course, sign out for lunch, sign back in after lunch and sign out at the end of the day. No, we did not have to wear ankle bracelets that signaled if we left the building. Nor did we need to have a monitor accompany us to the bathroom. What is the clear message? We can't be trusted to tell the Board that we did attend the lecture. I guess there would be too many people who would just pay and never attend the lecture. The assumption is if we are in the room we will be forced to be educated. Wrong!

Why then do these "continuing education" requirements exist? I have two hypotheses. By the way, psychologists always have hypotheses and not guesses. The first is the belief that you, the consumer, will feel more comfortable if you believe that we the psychologists are always aware of the newest techniques and laws. I will assure you that there is a great chance that some of the best therapists in the world have not changed how they do therapy in the last twenty years. I think this assumption has a whole lot more merit for physicians. I would not want to go into surgery with a physician who used the same operating techniques and equipment for the past twenty years.

The second hypothesis is that there is now a complete industry surrounding continuing education. Organizations are set up to offer classes for the rest of us. These organizations would all go bankrupt if the courses were optional.

After being in practice for thirty-seven years, there are few speakers I have any interest in hearing. There are few classes that can teach me anything new. I could learn completely new psychotherapy methods, but that would be like a dermatologist going to a continuing education lecture on proctology.

Every two years we are required to attend a four-hour class on laws and ethics. That is the class I am attending today. The substance of the class could be accomplished in about five minutes. Tell us the new laws that pertain to the practice of psychology that have been enacted in the last two years. However, these five minutes of new information gets spread over the entire four hours. I can give you a one-sentence summary of the content of most of these legal and ethical workshops: Do not screw your patients! This is meant literally and figuratively. It is fun sometimes to hear stories in these workshops of some of the outrageous and unethical things psychologists do. But, you probably read about most of them in the newspaper. What you don't hear about are some of the obscure regulations that psychologists have to follow. One example: It is required that every psychologist has a "notice to consumer" posted in their office that tells the patient who they can contact if there are any problems. This is mandatory. Confession number six: I have seen hundreds of psychologist offices and never once have I seen one of these notices posted. I sometimes have bad dreams of the consumer police taking me away in handcuffs in front of my patients.

I sit through the entire workshop but I think I would be a better therapist on Monday if I had spent the time playing golf.

October 7

Eight patients scheduled for today. This is generally the most patients I would see in one day. No cancellations and everyone shows up on time. At one p.m. I have a phone session with ST. ST is a lawyer, who I have seen in treatment for about three years. Seen in treatment isn't quite accurate. Initially, he lived and worked in Santa Monica and always came to the sessions in person. However, he moved about four hours away from L.A. about two years ago. He occasionally still drives in to see me, but most of our sessions are spent on the phone. I assume that any of the other two million therapists closer to him are just not good enough. Phone sessions definitely are not the same as in person sessions. Do you really know what the expression is on your therapist's face when you tell him something important? Trying to be empathic over the phone has its limitations. The patient can't even see my amazingly good eye contact, my concerned look or even my head shaking. As a person who likes to multi-task it is very difficult to do anything else when you have the patient live in front of you. My judgment says it would be very difficult to be checking my electronic organizer to see what tasks I have to do today. However, with a phone session multi-tasking becomes a reality. Check my organizer and listen at the same time; no problem. Listen and water my plants at the same time; no problem. Warning to all potential therapists!!! Do not lie down, close your eyes and try to listen at the same time. Confession number seven: I tried this once with a patient about seven years ago. Unfortunately, I did take a brief nap while the patient was talking. I was rudely awakened with the question: "What do you think of that?" There are times honesty can be very destructive. Telling the patient: "I am sorry I just missed the last five minutes because I was sleeping probably would have not gone over so well. Any patient who would continue to see his therapist at that point has serious problems and probably needs therapy. So, I revert to psychologist 101 skills. Everyone knows the skills. It is the art of turning every question into a question. "So, what do you think of that?" This is actually a skill that has been nurtured by my Jewish culture. "Mom, do I need a sweatshirt today? Son, what do you think?" Patients rarely get angry with this technique. Maybe they expect it from therapists. Therefore, it is a great way for a therapist to regain lost concentration.

October 8

I spend the first three hours of my day working at UCLA in the intensive treatment program for patients with severe OCD. Patients attend the program for four hours per day, five days per week for six weeks. It is a great program! People get better. My job is to supervise all of the behavioral treatment that goes on in the program. There are three therapists and some psychology students that I supervise. I have been with the program for about eight years. When I started in the program I was given the title of Director of Psychological Services by the medical director of the program. Unfortunately he never bothered to get any official approval for this position. Therefore, few people outside of the OCD program knew of my title. The way things work at places like UCLA is that you need signatures from about six to eight people in order to go to the bathroom. Today I encountered one of the administrators who basically told me that I couldn't have the title. Confession number eight: I will continue to call myself the Director of Psychological Services. I am afraid that one day that the title police will have me arrested. My biggest fear would be to lose one or more of my titles. It would be cruel indeed if they even took away the "D" from my Ph.D.

I have been associated with UCLA since 1978. Although it is an excellent academic institution it is one of the worst run businesses that you would ever want to see. The ability of the Neuropsychiatric Hospital to collect fees is pathetic. Often it will take them six to twelve months to bill patients for services. In 1986 my supervisor at UCLA informed me that in order for my position to continue to exist that I had to bill out for all the services I provided. After eight months of billing the administration informed me that I had billed out approximately $145,000. Unfortunately, UCLA only collected $2,500. Therefore, I was told that I was being "laid off." This reasoning has continued to puzzle me. Let's say I work in a shoe store. I sell a customer a new pair of shoes and the cashier neglects to ring up the sale. Who do you fire? If you said the shoe salesman, congratulations, you are now eligible to be employed in the billing department of UCLA.

October 11

I have five patients scheduled for today. My eleven a.m. patient, MN, is a movie producer. She is one of my favorite patients. Confession number nine: Therapists do have favorite and disliked patients. It is generally inadvisable to ask your therapist if you are his favorite patient. Generally you will get back a question such as: "Why is that important to you?" Even with my degree of honesty I doubt I would ever tell a patient that he or she is my favorite patient. I also do not think that my malpractice insurance covers my telling a patient they are my worst nightmare. Okay, I'm sure you want to know what makes my patient the "most favorite." (1) The patient always shows up on time and doesn't demand extra time at the end of the session. (2) The patient does all of the therapeutic assignments she is given. (3) The patient keeps reinforcing my therapy by telling me what a great job I am doing and how well the therapy is working. (4) The patient talks about interesting things during the session. I do not have to be daydreaming about other things. And (5) the patient pays all of her bills on time. Okay, so what makes a bad patient? (1) The patient arrives late for the session and demands to be seen past the end of the regularly scheduled time. (2) The patient continually comes up with excuses for not doing therapeutic assignments. (3) The patient has very little to say during the session. (4) The patient gets angry with the therapist. And (5) the patient pages you in the middle of the night and on weekends with non-emergency questions. For example, "Dr. Tarlow, I need to cancel my appointment for next week."

MN not only has all the qualities of a good patient, she occasionally goes overboard. She is the only patient I have had in the life of my practice who takes notes on her laptop during a session. Imagine how good I feel when all of my words of wisdom are being immediately written down. I wonder sometimes if she will be writing a book about her therapeutic experience. I sort of hope that my book comes out first.

October 11

I have five patients scheduled today. This is one of the worst days I have ever had in terms of patient's not showing up on time, or not showing up at all. My first patient is a no show. She never called to say she was not coming. Since her father pays for the treatment I doubt she cares about the cost of missing the session. My next patient shows up twenty minutes late. At least I get twenty-five minutes of therapy time with her. The next patient calls in and says he is sick and wants to have a phone session. I agree. However, there is a great deal of silence during the session. Maybe he is the one taking a nap this time. The following patient is another no show and no call. I had just met with him on Tuesday and given him an appointment card for Friday. Fridays in L.A. are generally horrible traffic days. Rush hour generally starts around two p.m. when I start seeing patients. I give most patients about fifteen minutes before I call them. Rarely do I ever get a hold of them. Occasionally I find them and tell them that I think we had an appointment scheduled. Most of the time they admit that they screwed up. However, occasionally some of them insist that I was wrong. I generally don't argue with the patient but I know I am right. Confession number ten: I told you I really liked no shows since I get paid for my time. However, I hate boredom even more. So, if I haven't brought enough reading material with me I can start to get really bored just sitting in my office waiting for patients to show up.

I get a call today from someone at the Dr. Phil show asking if I have any OCD patients who would be willing to come on the show. I call back and identify myself as Dr. Tarlow, although I really have an urge to tell them it is Dr. Jerry calling. Many of my patients ask me what they should call me. I tell them I have been practicing long enough that they can call me anything they want. It is okay to call me Jerry or Dr. Tarlow. However, I have never given them the option of calling me Dr. Jerry. That sounds fine for a six-year-old patient, not an adult.

Anyway, I ask the caller from the Dr. Phil show if they want me and my patients or just the patients. When they tell me just the patients I think to myself: Oh sure, I will gladly spend a few hours contacting patients for you to help out Dr. Phil. No way! Probably every therapist I know thinks they are better than Dr. Phil. So, we are all jealous that he gets to be on TV. I don't think I am going to help him.

October 14 – October 17

I decided about a month ago to schedule a short vacation for October. Four days off from seeing patients. The week before I leave on vacation I have to notify all of my patients that I won't be there the following week. It just wouldn't be cool for them to be waiting in my waiting room while I am sitting on the beach in Mexico. However, I often wonder how long they would sit there if I didn't come out to get them at the scheduled time. It might be interesting to do it as an experiment one week. And the winner is Jane Smith who waited four hours and seventeen minutes in my waiting room before deciding to go home.

Almost every patient asks where I am going. They all want to know whether it is business or pleasure. Many therapists never answer these questions. Some therapists still have the movie "What about Bob" in their head and believe that their patients would somehow follow them and ruin their vacations. I almost always answer their question about where I am going. I try to avoid answering questions about specific hotels since I do believe some patients would try to call me. Confession number eleven: I lie to patients when they ask me which hotel I am staying at. It is pleasant to not think about work for a few days.

I am on vacation with my wife, Nan. Nan is also a psychologist in private practice. Being married to a psychologist has some advantages. She definitely understands what I experience during a typical workday. She can actually help me with some of my problem cases. When my patients see her name on the office door (we share office space) they often ask me if that is my wife. As most patients know, just about everything said in a therapy session is confidential. Confession number twelve: Do not assume that any of the information you share with your therapist is kept confidential from your therapist's wife. Even if my wife were not a psychologist could you imagine me coming home at the end of the day and my wife greeting me: "Hi honey, how was your day?" "Great dear. I had this very famous patient today, but I can't tell you his name or what his problem is." I just don't think that would fly with too many spouses. This is not the CIA. However, I do believe you have to trust your spouse to not tell other people.

One of the truly great things about my vacations is that I am not on call. I don't have to take my pager with me or even pick up any of my messages. One of the truly horrible things about vacations is picking up my messages on the day that I get home. The answering machine usually sounds like this: "You have thirty-two new messages." Often I don't get much sleep the last night of vacation. I have this recurring nightmare of calling my answering machine when I get back and hearing: "You have 476 new messages." I wake up screaming and have difficulty getting back to sleep.

When I am away on vacation another psychologist will usually cover for me in emergencies. I have some difficulty with this concept. I have a hard time imagining a patient I have seen for a year calling a therapist he has never seen at a critical time. But, some patients actually do this. I do keep score of how many patients call me when I cover for other therapists.

The other horrible thing about returning from vacation is picking up the week's mail at the office. Usually, I need a full day to return calls and open up all the mail. It sometimes seems like all of the great stress management benefits from the vacation can be lost in the course of twenty-four hours. If I were a patient I would not schedule an appointment with my therapist on the therapist's first day back from vacation.

October 18

It is my first day back from vacation. I only have scheduled two hours at UCLA, one hour of supervision, and two patient hours. This will give me enough time to return the thirty-two phone calls I have received the previous four days. Many of these phone calls are from new patients. A typical message goes something like: "Dr. Tarlow, I got your name from Dr. Referral who told me you specialize in treating fear of flying. I need to make an appointment. Can you see me next Monday at one p.m.? Please call." Some people have a wonderful sense of entitlement or believe that the doctor they have just called has unlimited openings. Here is some free advice. If your doctor calls back and can see you at the exact time you asked for, do not bother making the appointment because he is likely not busy enough to be any good.

One of my favorite types of message comes from the new patient who spends four minutes talking to the answering machine about his problems and then forgets to leave a phone number. Another favorite is the patient who forgets to leave his name. When I return these calls I sometimes want to say to the person who answers the phone: "This is Dr. Tarlow. Is there someone at this number who may have called me because they are having psychological problems?" I envision everyone in the family getting on the phone to try and figure out whose problems are worse.

When I return these calls some people try to get a full session over the phone. They want to tell you their life history, all of their problems and all of the treatment they have had. I have the desire to ask some of them what their favorite movie and TV shows are. Cutting people off is sometimes difficult. I have to listen to them long enough so that they know I am a caring therapist. Therefore, I try to return most of these calls a few minutes before the hour so that I can tell them that I have a patient waiting and have to get off the phone, but if they would like to make an appointment I would be glad to schedule it now. Confession number thirteen: Many times there is no patient waiting.

October 21

I have nine patients scheduled today. It is truly my first day back from vacation. My first patient is another one of my favorites. He is generally a good patient to start the week off with. He starts the session by asking me how my vacation was. This in itself is a good therapeutic sign. He realizes that I was away the previous week. This question actually leads to a ten-minute discussion of my vacation. Now, it is a generally accepted therapeutic principle that the therapist does not give the patient any direct advice. For example, it would be inappropriate for the therapist to tell the patient to sell all of her shares of United Airlines because the therapist just sold all of his. Confession number fourteen: There are times when I have a tremendous need for demonstrating to a patient that I have found a bargain that even my Jewish mother would have been proud of. Today was such a time. I couldn't help myself. I actually think this increases my value in the eyes of certain patients. No, I did not tell my patient what stock to sell. I did tell him about an incredible timeshare that I bought. And yes, it was a bargain.

One of the other qualities I like about this patient is his sense of humor. I can actually make a joke and he laughs. Some patients resent their therapist's attempt at humor. I even had one patient who thought I was mocking him every time I smiled. I would practice keeping a straight face prior to each session. After he left I would break up laughing. I still believe that repressed laughter is bad for your health.

One final thing I like about this patient. He is a clock-watcher. He constantly checks to see how much time remains in the session. He always starts to write his check three to five minutes prior to the end of the session. I really enjoy not being the one watching the clock. I have three clocks strategically place in my office. I try to glance at one of them when the patient is not looking. Some patients occasionally catch me. They seldom say anything, but occasionally they give me a dirty look.

October 22

I spend three hours at UCLA and then I have six patients scheduled. Let's talk about boring patients. My one p.m. patient is extremely depressed. He is also boring. Paying attention to a boring patient is difficult. The first skill one needs to develop is the ability to either daydream or problem solve when the patient is talking. Since my last vacation was just the past week it is easy to daydream about being on the beach in Mexico.

The second skill is learning how to hide a yawn. Patients do not need to know that their therapist's think they are boring. I practice yawning with my mouth shut, with my hand over my mouth and I try to sneak them in when the patient is not looking at me. There are times the patient quickly looks up and catches me in a yawn. That is embarrassing. Again, most patients are not assertive enough to say anything.

I try to maximize the chances of my staying awake during the session. One thing that helps me is keeping the temperature of my office very cold. Unfortunately, many patients enter the office and immediately comment on the temperature. They want to know if I could lend them a ski jacket. I empathize with them and go over to the thermostat to change the temperature. Confession number fifteen: I pretend to change the temperature on the thermostat, but most of the time I leave it where it is set. I then tell the patient it will take a few minutes for the new temperature to kick in. Few patients continue to complain.

My drug of choice for staying awake is caffeine. Unfortunately, I do not drink coffee. I therefore tend to consume large quantities of diet Pepsi during my sessions. This helps keep me awake. However, I now have to get to the bathroom after each session. There are times I have doubted I would make it through the session. After many years I believe I have conditioned my bladder to last for the entire forty-five-minute session.

The final technique for staying awake is movement. I cross my legs, I uncross my legs, I get up to hand the patient a paper, I get up to demonstrate something to the patient, I get up to change the thermostat, I get up to close the blinds, I get up to turn on a light etc. There are times I wish I could ask the patient to have the session during a brisk walk. That would definitely keep me awake, and I could window shop at the same time!

October 24

A very easy day. I only have three patients scheduled, and one of them is my favorite patient. I notice that my fees vary for each of the three patients. I realize that I keep raising my fees every few months. I wonder if I am trying to price myself out of business, or see just how much people will pay to see me. I have purposely taken myself off all insurance company lists of preferred providers. They tend to pay from one-third to one-half of my normal fees. Insurance companies pay the same amount to all psychologists on their lists regardless of specialties, board certifications or years of experience. I was not raised with this type of mentality. I believe you should pay more for a specialist and more for someone who has twenty years of experience vs. someone who just received his license. Can you imagine being arrested and having to hire a criminal attorney? Here is your choice: Jeffery Attorney has tried 2000 criminal cases and has been in practice for twenty years, or Ralph Lawyer who just passed the bar last week. Would expect to pay the same for both attorneys? That is the way some of the insurance companies think. That is also one of the reasons why the vast majority of good therapists are not on any insurance preferred provider lists. There are times in this city when I would like to adjust my fees based on the income of the patient. I know some patients really struggle to pay my fee and other patients wouldn't care if I charged $500 an hour. You may wonder how I go about setting my fee. I simply look at the average fee of a mediocre attorney and divide it in half. I cannot actually tell you how much I charge, because by the time this book is printed I probably will have raised my fees several times. Confession number sixteen: I charge a lot. I'm not sure that I would pay that much to see me if I had a psychological problem. Some therapists I know actually dedicate their furniture to certain patients. "Did you see my new couch? That is courtesy of my one p.m. patient."

Certain patients try to bargain for their fee. "Is there any way you could reduce your fee?" Sometimes I just don't get these requests. I tried doing it in Ralph's supermarket last week when I was checking out. I said to the checker: "I know my food bill comes to $145. I was wondering if you would take $100?" She looked at me as if I needed psychiatric help. I will say that there are certain cultures that tend to try to bargain more than others. For the sake of not being called a racist, I will not reveal which ones.

I try to collect my fees from patients at the end of each session. After years of billing patients and having some patients never pay, I decided to collect at each session. This has drastically increased my collections. Several patients who I have billed have told me they were not going to pay because they didn't improve enough. Keep in mind, psychotherapy generally has no guarantees. There is one guarantee that

I make to my patients. I guarantee them that if they don't do the work I ask them to do that they will not get better. There is no paragraph in my office policy that states: "If for any reason you are unhappy with your treatment, or the amount of improvement, I will refund your money completely." I am not running a department store.

I try not to raise the fees of patients I had begun seeing at a lower fee. This tends to be a difficult policy to maintain for the patients that I have seen for thirteen years. However, I sometimes ask myself if I will work as hard for someone paying a lot less than my new patients.

October 25

Well, the title police at UCLA have become more persistent. I was told this week that I could not have the title of a director of a program since no one else in the entire University system has a title if they are not on salary from UCLA. This edict came from a psychiatrist who has some vague administrative position in the Department of Psychiatry at UCLA. This psychiatrist and I are not exactly good buddies. He has wanted me removed from my position for many years even though the OCD program is generally considered one of the best in the country and I have not cost the University one cent in salary during the past seven years. Confession number seventeen: I would like to write this psychiatrist a memo telling him what an ignorant, incompetent ass he is. However, I don't do it because I am unsure that he can read since he has never responded to any of the memos I have sent him. How does a professional in your own department do that? I never find myself thinking: "Oh, that memo is from Dr. Obnoxious so I won't call him back."

So, after being told that I could no longer keep my title I did what any self-respecting child would do. I took my toys and went home. That means I told the Medical Director of the program that I would no longer do about eight jobs that I have been doing for free for the past eight years.

At UCLA many of the people who are academic faculty are actually in charge of budgets. These people were not trained to do these things. Let me give you one example. The OCD Program at UCLA can only admit two patients for each therapist in the program. Currently we have three therapists, since one therapist resigned last December. We also have a waiting list of patients willing to come into the program and pay $330 per day. However, we have been unable to replace the therapist who resigned. The program therefore loses about twenty-five percent of its possible revenue. If I ran a company and someone under my supervision did not replace an employee who resigned and the company income fell 25 percent, I would fire the person responsible for not replacing the employee. That never happens at UCLA. First of all, it is difficult to really determine who is responsible. Then, the person responsible is often a tenured faculty who can't be fired.

I will continue to work at UCLA in the capacity of an Associate Clinical Professor. They have not taken that title away from me yet. However, after reading this book, it is a distinct possibility that I will be asked to resign from the faculty.

October 28

I have seven patients scheduled today. My twelve p.m. patient EP has been in therapy for about 10 weeks. She has panic attacks. Panic attacks are very interesting phenomena. Imagine for a second that you are walking across the street and you turn to see a car racing toward you and you think the car is going to hit you. Now, imagine having that feeling for thirty minutes without stopping. I think that is what a panic attack feels like. It is sometimes hard for me to relate to some of my anxious patients. I am not an anxious person. Many of my patients want to know if I ever had a panic attack. I think some of them believe that all therapists should be like the majority of addiction counselors. That is, most addiction counselors seem to be ex-addicts. I try to tell some of them that I become anxious on the top of extremely steep ski runs, but I don't think that is what they are looking for. Many of them are then intrigued by the fact that I am treating anxiety disorders and never had one. So, the logical next question often is: "Why did you get into this field?" The answer is actually very simple. Psychology is interesting. Figuring out how to change human behavior is challenging. You do not have to be emotionally disturbed to be a therapist. It is not a prerequisite for graduate school. The faculty in charge of admissions did not say: "We can't accept Tarlow into our program because he has never had a serious depression and his parents were actually nice to him."

Getting back to EP. This patient is almost done with treatment. She is no longer having panic attacks and will be returning to work within the next two weeks. Confession number eighteen: It is very important to me that my patients get better. I keep score. My "cure" rate definitely has to exceed seventy percent in order for me to feel good. It is hard for me to imagine working day after day, week after week and not see my patients get better.

October 29

I'll see four patients today. Two people canceled at the last minute. My three p.m. patient is FG. FG is a depressed twenty-nine-year-old single female who recently moved from New York. She starts the session complaining about L.A. This is difficult for me to listen to. It is nearly November and she is wearing shorts. I wonder how she would be dressed in New York. After five minutes of listening to her complaints I am forced to defend the city that I have lived in for the past thirty-five years. I don't like negativity. No wonder FG is depressed. She is a learned pessimist.

Depressed patients are definitely more work than anxious patients. Some of them just drain all of the energy and happiness from any room they enter. The very nature of depression makes it unlikely that that the patient is willing to do much work to get over the depression. Very often depressed patients have little to say in a session. Many therapists expect long periods of silence. Many therapists are trained to sit there silently staring back at the patient. Confession number nineteen: I can't keep my mouth shut during the therapy session. I can tolerate about thirty to forty-five seconds of silence before I have to say something. I once had a patient who had something to say for about the first five to ten minutes of the session. After that it was mostly silence. After putting up with his behavior for a long time I finally interrupted one of his silences by telling him he was not at all prepared for the therapy session and he had to go back in the waiting room and think about what he wanted to talk about for the remainder of the session. This was the first time I ever tried this with a patient.

Unfortunately, this technique backfired completely. The patient did not return to the waiting room. Instead he left the building and phoned me a day later telling me he was quitting therapy. I have not tried this technique since then.

October 31

I have four patients scheduled today. My nine a.m. patient is GJ. GJ is a flying phobic. He has not flown since 1994. He was self-referred after seeing me on television talking about a new treatment for fear of flying: virtual reality therapy (VR therapy). VR therapy is something I started offering a few years ago in an attempt to utilize an exciting new technology in order to help make me rich and cure thousands of patients. Psychologists also have fantasies of "hitting it big." A colleague and I invested in the equipment in order to become the first therapists in L.A. to offer VR therapy. After setting up the equipment and hiring a public relations firm we waited patiently for our massive TV appearances and then the influx of referrals. The first year we managed to get two TV interviews and one article in a small newspaper. Although the treatment has been extremely effective, people are not breaking down our doors to cure their flying fears. I think that many people are using the tragedy of September 11 to justify the fact that they shouldn't fly.

GJ is actually completing the treatment today after only eight sessions. He then has to take a real flight to realize the treatment is effective. VR therapy is likely to become more and more popular in the coming years. My favorite VR program is the one that helps to treat fear of public speaking. It puts the patient in a virtual auditorium where the therapist can control the actions of the audience. If the speech is good the therapist can have the audience applaud. If it is boring the therapist can have the audience yawn or fall asleep. I am afraid that this program might one day be combined with some of my son's video games. "Hey Dad, that guy's speech was really boring so I blew him away with my AK47."

I think the possibilities for virtual reality therapy are unlimited. Even though all of the applications currently center on anxiety disorders, I think that VR could be really useful for helping people with anger issues. How about the virtual teenager program? You practice arguing with an uncooperative teenager. How about a virtual New York City driving program where someone cuts you off while you are driving, gives you the finger and then starts swearing at you? I also would like to see the virtual repair service phone call. You call to get your washer repaired and you are put on hold for twenty minutes while listening to muzak. The possibilities are just endless.

CHAPTER 2
November

November 1

My three p.m. patient TU is one of my least favorites. She is extremely serious and never smiles. I see her every other week. She has cancelled the last five or six sessions in a row. She always waits until the last minute to cancel, usually twenty-four-and-a half hours before her appointment. She is smart enough to remember that she will be charged for the appointment if she cancels any later. But, she is inconsiderate enough to hardly ever give me more than twenty-five hours to find a replacement.

TU tells me that today she needs to talk about one specific issue. She believes that when she is sleeping she pokes her finger in her ear repeatedly and this may eventually cause hearing loss. Let's just say this is not the most common problem people bring into therapy. In fact, in my thirty-two years of practice, she is the first. This brings up an interesting issue. What happens when a patient asks you if you have experience treating this problem? Confession number twenty: I lie to my patients. I almost always tell them that I have heard of the problem or that I have had other patients with the same problem. The patient does not want to know that she is the only person in the world with the problem. Luckily, TU does not ask this question. However, I have to figure out a treatment plan to deal with this problem. It is clear that TU just wants to view it as a bad habit; like people who bite their nails.

Okay, so I decide to go along with this idea. One of the treatments for bad habits is called stimulus control. All this means is that you have to arrange the environment to minimize the occurrence of the problem. So, after twenty years of school, a Ph.D. in Clinical Psychology and all these years of practice I am advising a patient to wear mittens and ear muffs to sleep so that she can't stick her finger in her ear. Brilliant! Maybe I should write this up as a case study for a journal. After all, who knows how many other people are suffering needlessly from this problem?

November 4

My one o'clock patient HJ has been coming to see me for over a year. He has OCD and depression. He is the only patient I currently see whose treatment is paid for by a managed care company. As I mentioned earlier, I have removed my name from all insurance lists. This patient was assertive enough to insist that he wanted to be treated by an expert in OCD. When this happens the insurance company generally tries to convince the patient that they can find him an expert who is on their panel. Please note: this is bullshit. If there were an expert on their panel why would he accept less than fifty percent of his normal fee to see a patient? The insurance company believes that if the practitioner stated in his application that he was experienced in seeing OCD patients, it must be true. No provider insurance application asks for the number of patients you have seen with a particular diagnosis.

After my patient contacted the insurance company I received a very pleasant call from a case manager asking me if I would sign a single-case agreement to see this particular patient for the insurance company. I told them I would be happy to sign the agreement if it was for my normal rate. After letting them know my rate there is generally a long pause and they tell me they have to get back to me. They tell me they don't know if the company will approve such a high rate. I then inform them that they have already done this for a previous patient. This does put them in a very bad position. How do they turn me down for the current patient if they have previously approved my rate for another patient? A few days later I get a call from the insurance company approving my rate. They then ask me if I would like to be on their panel officially. Let me try to get across the absurdity of this question. Suppose you could convince your boss to give you a pay raise that would double your pay. Now, suppose your boss came to you and said "Ralph, how would you like to sign a document ensuring that from now on all your paychecks will be only fifty percent of what you are now making?" I'm sure everyone just jumps at this type of opportunity.

Even if I get paid my normal fee, I find that the paperwork for the insurance company is ridiculous. My file on this patient is about five inches thick. Every five weeks I have to contact the insurance company to get approval for more sessions and I have to justify it to some company employee who has never seen the patient and who probably has about 20 years less experience than I do. They generally only care about saving the company money. Managed care for psychological treatments is a disaster. Patient care suffers and therapists become employees of the insurance company, making less money. Confession number twenty-one: I hate managed care companies and their employees.

November 5

Like anyone else these days I get e-mails. Some of my patients ask for my e-mail address and feel more comfortable sending me e-mails than leaving messages on my answering machine. So now I have one more thing to check every day. My name must also be on a number of e-mail lists of providers for OCD and anxiety disorders. One of the things today's consumer of mental health services can do is to send the same e-mail to thousands of providers. They can then choose to see the provider that best answers their questions. Many of these questions do tend to be inappropriate. For example: "I have been taking 20 mg. of Prozac for the past year. I have recently developed a bad head cold. Should I stop taking my Prozac?" I assume the patient thought I was a psychiatrist. I tend not to answer these types of e-mails.

Today's e-mail may have been the best I ever received. It was unsolicited and from a person I have never met or talked to. It is important that you not have anything in your mouth when you read this. "to be honest my head is messed I need get over my probs i cant take prozac makes me not eat for a week. i cant take clomipramine. i shake and feel real messy, im over in the uk im wonderin if i do take prozac is there anythin on earth i can take aswell to make me want to eat or want to have an appetite i need get over this cos believe me mine is a case alot diff to others, ive got the good and badluck thing. That really riles me."

I am amazed that this individual can correctly spell the drug clomipramine but virtually nothing else.

The very same day another e-mail arrives. "Dear Mr. Tarlow, My name is Stanley, I'm from Belgium. Since one year I have to swallow my saliva every 10 to 15 seconds. My psychiatrist sais it was some type of OCD. Could you give me some tips. Thanks" Here is what I would like to write back to Stanley. "Dear Stanley: My first tip for you is that when you contact a psychologist you call him Dr., not Mr. My second tip is that the way to spell 'says' is says. My third tip is to go back to school to help you with your English grammar. Finally, as far as the saliva is concerned please call my office for an appointment as soon as you get to L.A." Confession number twenty-two: I return every call that is left on my answering machine, no matter how absurd the message. The message is left for me personally, not electronically generated to hundreds of therapists. I do not respond to most of the unusual e-mails.

November 7

I have an interview scheduled for TV news today. They want to do a piece on the VR flying therapy. I look at my presence on the news as free marketing. Every time I appear I seem to get calls from many new patients. The first problem I have is what to wear. I generally dress for work in nice slacks and a dress shirt. I never wear a tie or jacket during a regular therapy day. I do want to look professional, but not at the cost of being uncomfortable. I have some colleagues who dress in jeans and sandals. Even though I would be more physically comfortable wearing jeans and tennis shoes, I would feel particularly embarrassed when patients would see me dressed like that. My two exceptions to the tie and jacket rule are job interviews and TV appearances. I have often wondered what the people who hired me thought after I started a new job and never again showed up in a tie and jacket. I have always thought it would be to my advantage to wear my one suit to

TV interviews. Having one suit only becomes a problem if there are multiple interviews in the same week. The TV interview lasts about ninety minutes. My guess is that I will be on TV for about thirty seconds. The reporters are fascinated by the VR therapy. They want to run the piece during sweeps week.

My last patient of the day is TN. TN is an interesting patient. He was actually convicted of sexually exhibiting himself in public. Part of his probation involved receiving several hours of therapy per week. In my experience, patients who are court ordered for therapy rarely are motivated to change. They are very motivated to stay out of jail or prison so they do show up consistently for their appointments. I sometimes imagine the judge asking the patient: "Here is your choice: two years in prison or two years with a shrink." I then imagine the patient hesitating before making the decision. I actually believe TN is motivated to change.

After dealing with so many patients with anxiety disorders every day it is almost refreshing to talk about sex. Besides the exhibitionism problem, TN also has a foot fetish. I have some difficulty listening to a patient talk about being turned on by foot odor. These sorts of problems reinforce my belief in learning theory. I believe people can learn to become sexually excited by almost anything. When I was in graduate school, the first real clinical experience I had was as a therapist in the Montana State Prison. During one session an inmate confided in me that he was having a relationship with a sheep. To this day I still do not know if he was serious or just taking advantage of a young student's naiveté.

One of my goals with TN has been to get him to have a "normal" sexual relationship, or at least a relationship that won't get him arrested. In order to get to this point he needs to learn certain social skills and learn to not be anxious in social situations with women. After teaching him these skills in the first three months of therapy, I realize that I have twenty-one more court ordered months to see this patient.

November 8

I'm actually a bit under the weather today. In fact I had a 101degree fever last night and felt miserable. I must make a decision of whether I want to cancel all my patients and stay in bed all day or go to work sick. One of the problems with being in private practice is that I really do not have any sick days. I can take off as many days as I want, but I won't get paid. I think this is a little unfair. When I worked as a psychologist for UCLA I would always get paid for being sick. Somehow I don't think this concept would go over very well with patients. I could call my patients and say, "This is Dr. Tarlow. I'm really feeling sick today so I won't be coming in. It's okay if you just mail me the check for today's session." There have been a few times over the years that I have felt sick enough to cancel all my patients for a day. I have had several sarcastic patients tell me that I did not give them twenty-four-hour notice.

After realizing that staying in bed and watching TV is not a whole lot different from sitting in my office chair and listening to patients, I decide to go to work. The only times I am really forced to cancel patients is when I have laryngitis and can't talk. I am sure most patients don't like the fact that their therapist isn't feeling a hundred percent healthy. There are a number of my OCD patients who would be horrified by all the germs I am bringing into the office.

When I go to work feeling sick it often makes me think of how I feel when a patient comes to the session and is obviously physically ill. Now, I don't have OCD, but being in an enclosed room with a patient violently coughing, sneezing, and blowing her nose does not make me smile. Some of these patients come to the session because they know they will be charged since they didn't cancel with twenty-four-hour notice. Others come to the session because they are so narcissistic that they don't care they are infecting everyone else. Confession number twenty-three: I will waive my twenty-four-hour notice policy if a patient calls up and tells me how sick they are. You may want to try this with your therapist. "Dr. Gullible, I know I have a two p.m. appointment today, but I am coughing and sneezing all the time. Do you still want me to come in?" Now the therapist must decide if it is worth the fee to have you in his office.

By the time I get to the office I am actually feeling a bit better. No patients suspect that I have been sick. I am able to get through the day. There probably aren't many jobs that I could have done today.

November 11

It is Veteran's Day, an official holiday. Most people aren't working. Just about all of my patients want to come in today. The topic of the day seems to be how people exaggerate the meaning of physical sensations they are experiencing. There are times when it seems like I say the same thing to many different patients during the day. I have some OCD patients who are obsessed with their physical health. They worry that every physical symptom is very serious and they must go to the doctor right away. I have panic patients who feel a physical symptom such as their heart beating fast and think they are having a heart attack. I have patients that are phobic about going to doctors because they believe they will be diagnosed with some horrible disease. I also have patients who fear they might get a horrible disease from being around others who have a disease, such as cancer. Finally, I have patients who obsess about dying from some horrible disease. Six of the eight patients I saw today have one or more of these thoughts.

November 12

I generally only see adult patients. There are several reasons for this. I was never really trained in child psychology and often children and adolescents are brought in by their parents and do not want to be in therapy. Many parents view this process similar to car repairs. "I am leaving Johnny with you. Please repair him and tell me when I can pick him up." Many children have difficulty relating to therapists and tend to be very non-communicative during the session. They also frequently have difficulty completing therapeutic assignments. I don't know if it would be better to grade them as though they were in school. So, I have arbitrarily set a minimum age limit of seventeen on my patients. I must admit I occasionally break my own rule and treat someone younger. I have one such patient today.

MP is a fifteen-year-old that I have been seeing for about three months. I agreed to see her on the request of her father who used to be married to a friend of mine. Confession number twenty-four: Flattery will get you everywhere. Just like anyone else I am vulnerable to intense flattery. This patient's father insisted that I see his daughter, because I was the best! After resisting for all of two minutes, I caved in and agreed to see her.

MP is a very bright kid who goes to one of the best private schools in L.A. She has OCD that centers on perfectionism, especially in her schoolwork. Now I know that most parents would jump for joy if their child spent many hours on schoolwork. But believe me there are limits to how many times a paper can be rewritten. After successfully treating her OCD within a few months, MP has continued to come to sessions to talk about other "issues." Included in these issues is her use of drugs and her relationship with her parents. During one session she suggests that marijuana is more effective in treating her problems than Prozac. After all, she reasons, it makes her feel better. She has actually been given permission by her parents to smoke marijuana one time per week at home. I have some serious problems with this approach but I am reluctant to call her parents and break confidentiality. But how naive can the parents be to assume that their daughter will stick to smoking just one time per week?

Today MP was asking me questions about colleges. She was trying to get feedback on the rankings of colleges according to the magazine "High Times." One of the interesting things about seeing a fifteen-year-old daughter is to hear what I have to look forward to with my own thirteen-year-old child. It is scary! I guess I also compare my parenting skills to her parents'. It has long been a stereotype that the child of a therapist is likely to be very "screwed up." If that were so, imagine what the chances of mental health should be for my son, the child of two therapists. So far I think my child is a normal, mentally healthy teenager. I am keeping my fingers crossed.

November 14

I have a new female patient today. SM is a 32-year-old single woman who is having severe panic disorder. I have treated so many patients for panic disorder that I sometimes feel bored repeating the same things over and over again, even if I know the techniques are effective. SM has no chance of boring me since she is one of the most attractive women I have ever treated. This is a patient I should see at four in the afternoon when I am usually ready to take a nap. Confession number twenty-five: I am more attentive and animated when I see attractive female patients. This does not mean that I want to have sex with them. I think it is sort of a conditioned reaction from years of non-therapy male-female interactions. I am proud to say I have never dated or socialized with a patient outside of the therapy situation. However, it is easy to see how sex with a patient could occur. I have had several patients make somewhat overt passes at me. I have also had one patient lie about her interactions with me. I believe she did this to try to blackmail me and get back all of the money she had paid for therapy. One of the things she told her attorney was that I offered her a drink during the session. Since the only drinks I have in my office are water and soda I was amazed at this accusation. She also told her attorney that I had sessions with her "late at night." That was true. I saw her at seven p.m., which has been my last scheduled appointment for the past fifteen years. As many stories as you may have heard about a therapist having sex with a patient, what you haven't heard about is the hundreds of times patients falsely accuse therapists. The sad thing about this is that most therapists will gladly refund the patient's money rather than take the issue to court. It hurts sometimes to be right, but it's financially irresponsible to fight for the principle.

I have had several attractive female patients who dressed very provocatively for their sessions. Since I am not a psychoanalyst I do not have to interpret this behavior. My only problem is sometimes maintaining appropriate eye contact. I wonder if my wife ever has the same problem with attractive male patients. I have never asked her.

November 15 and November 16

Occasionally I go to psychology conferences. There are very few conferences that I am ever interested in attending. The topics presented in the conference have to be relevant to my clinical practice and the conference has to be located in a city I am interested in visiting. For example, if the annual conference of the Anxiety Disorders Association of America was held in Fargo there would be no way I would attend. Move it to Maui and I am there for the whole week. The conference this week is in Reno. Since I used to work in Reno, I still have several friends I can visit and therefore I decided to attend the conference.

I hardly ever go to a conference without presenting a paper or giving a workshop. For this conference I have gathered together a group of people who have been working with OCD patients and have agreed to participate in a "clinical roundtable" discussion of treatment resistant OCD. This will take place on Saturday.

I have attended psychology conferences for over thirty years. When you register for the conference you get an identification badge. I always noticed that some people received badges that had ribbons attached to them. These ribbons generally indicated some sort of status or special position within the organization. When I go to pick up my registration materials I find that for the first time in my life I have ribbons. Two ribbons. One for being a diplomate in behavior therapy from ABPP and the other for being a "fellow." Confession number twenty-six: I generally never wear convention badges because the pin usually makes a hole in my shirt or coat. Today I will wear my badge. I HAVE RIBBONS!! I want to make sure that everyone sees that I have ribbons. I probably spent extra time walking around the hotel to make sure that everyone sees that I have ribbons. This behavior sounds appropriate-for a ten year old.

Since I am at the convention I decide to sit in on a few lectures and see if I actually can learn something new or at least hear a "famous" psychologist speak. I am generally disappointed in these talks. Today is no exception. I spend three hours in a workshop that was supposed to be about new treatments for obsessions. The title would have been accurate if they removed the word "new." I am impressed by the sophistication of the questions from the audience and realize that probably half of the hundred people in the audience could have taught this workshop. I know I could have. I decide that three hours at the convention is more than enough for one day so I leave to go play tennis in the afternoon and visit with friends.

On Saturday I am scheduled to give my "talk." I usually enjoy presenting papers at conferences. Since I am so difficult to please as an audience member, I strive to give an entertaining and informative talk. It is important to me to get the audience to laugh at least a few times. My biggest fear is that no one will show up for my talk. Today, I have learned that the official program of the convention did not list my talk in the correct room. The correction was published in an "addendum" to the program and distributed along with twenty other papers to registrants when they checked in to the convention. No one reads these addendums! My worst fear has materialized. There are five presenters ready to present and a total of three people in the audience. Even having ribbons at this point doesn't make me feel better. I am somewhat intolerant of incompetence. I cannot believe that the program committee didn't know that no one would show up. This must have happened before. If they had informed me when the original program came out I probably would have told them to cancel the talk. We do end up having a nice cozy discussion among the people present.

I decide to attend two other talks on Saturday afternoon. One talk, given by a famous psychologist, is a waste of two hours. However, at the presidential address the incoming president of the organization gives an excellent talk on social anxiety disorder. I actually learn two or three things that I didn't know. As a bonus this information will actually help me in my practice. I now consider my attendance at the convention a partial success. I saw my friends, I learned a few new things and I got ribbons.

November 18

I have eight patients scheduled today and I will have some difficulty getting through the day. Confession number twenty-seven: Although I may have told you that I don't really get anxious, I lied a little. I do have some social anxiety. I definitely do not want to feel embarrassed in public. I think this anxiety is probably typical for most people, even therapists. Today, as I entered my office one of my colleagues told me that I had a giant rip down the back of my pants. I obviously did not see this when I got dressed in the morning. I try using scotch tape to hold the tear together and that helps some. I now have to see all my patients without any of them seeing my behind. It might be interesting to actually let them see the rip and see how many of them would say anything. But, I prefer to try to hide this from them for the entire day.

My three o'clock patient, ME, is an old patient that I see about two or three times a year. She calls me every time her OCD flares up and the techniques I have taught her are not working. One of her OCD symptoms is very unique. She believes that there are signs on her body. These signs, sort of like post-its, say not very nice things about her. She used to believe there were signs that said she was a child molester. Today she believes she has a sign that says she is frigid. This now becomes a problem with social anxiety because she believes others are able to see these signs. After hearing about everything that she has tried to do that failed, I come to the conclusion after fifteen minutes of therapy that the best assignment for her is to actually go out and have sex. I start to put her folder away as if I am done with the session, but she does not believe the treatment could be that simple. I believe, though, that it may act as a reassurance for her. At one point in his treatment I had her do exposure assignments where she actually wrote the feared message on herself or on a small post-it. These assignments seemed to work well in decreasing her anxiety.

November 19

There are certain behaviors patients do that tend to annoy me. Answering cell phones during the session is one such behavior. Before cell phones, it was only the therapist who needed to make a decision as to whether or not to answer the phone. Most therapists would simply turn the ringer off on their phone or not pick it up when it rings. Occasionally, you could find a therapist who actually answers the phone when they are in the middle of a session with a patient. I never really understood this behavior. The therapist, of course, does this without permission of the patient. I guess it would sound a little awkward to ask the patient: "I know you are paying for my time, but I hope you don't mind if I answer that call." Since I have never done this I am not sure what goes through the mind of a therapist who does answer the phone. I guess a few possibilities are; (1) I think someone more important is calling; (2) I think someone with more pressing problems is calling, or (3) You couldn't possibly be assertive enough to tell me not to answer the call. If I were a patient and my therapist answered a routine phone call I would walk out of the office and never come back!

These days about ninety percent of my patients have cell phones. Most of them decide to leave them on during the session. Frequently the cell phones ring, or what is more common these days play a song. Patients often look at the caller ID and then determine if they want to take the call or continue talking to the therapist. After all, it is their time and if they want to use it to talk to their friend during the session, so be it. Most patients who answer the phone do tell the other party the truth. "I am at my shrink's office. Can I call you back in thirty-seven minutes?" Confession number twenty-eight: It is truly annoying to have a patient talk on their cell phone for more than thirty seconds. I sometimes start to do other things like get a glass of water, do paperwork, or even go to the bathroom. One day I would like to start returning calls while the patient is talking on the phone. I am not sure what they expect me to be doing while they talk on the phone. I often have the urge to grab the phone out of their hands and ask the person on the line if they would like to have a group therapy session.

November 21

Another relatively easy day today; just four patients scheduled. I have a meeting today with the real estate agent about renewing my lease in the building. There are certain features of my Calabasas office that I find problematic. The first is that there is very bad soundproofing in the walls. This makes for an interesting problem when two therapists are seeing patients at the same time. Having a hysterical patient in one office can tend to be disturbing to the people in the next office. There have been times my patient actually has become very quiet in order to eavesdrop on the conversation in the other office. The worst problem with soundproofing occurs when one therapist is using the virtual reality equipment and another therapist is seeing a patient in his office. Have you ever tried to do psychotherapy with a 747 taking off in the next room? It can be quite distracting.

Another problem is that there is no separate exit door. Therefore, patients must exit through the waiting room and sometimes see the next patient waiting. Some therapy patients require complete confidentiality and do not want anyone to know they are seeing a psychologist. I actually had one famous patient ask to enter through the exit door so that other patients wouldn't see her in the waiting room. In one of the buildings where I used to work, there were always famous people in the elevators. My colleagues and I used to have fun guessing which therapist the person was seeing and speculating on the diagnosis.

The biggest problem of not having an exit door is that if I need to go the bathroom before my next patient I have to walk through the waiting room where the patient is seated. Upon seeing me most patients assume I have come to get them to start the session. Confession number twenty-nine: I never start a session early. I always return from the bathroom and tell the patient I will see her in a few minutes after I return a phone call.

November 22

I have a new patient scheduled for today. Part of my job is to actually sell myself to new patients on the phone. Since my rates are high it is important for me to "convert" the initial phone call into an appointment. I generally try to convince the new patient that I have a great deal of experience in dealing with the problem he or she is presenting. Confession number thirty: I always tell patients I am very experienced with the problem they are presenting, no matter what the problem is. I always tell patients I have seen many other people with similar problems. "Dr. Tarlow, have you ever heard of anyone being afraid of her shadow?" "Of course I have. I have probably treated more of these cases than anyone in California." "Dr. Tarlow, have you ever heard of anyone thinking he had turned into a chocolate chip cookie?" "Of course I have. Just last month I treated someone with the exact same problem." Patients want to know they are not unique. Patients want to know that their therapist is an expert with their problem.

I tend to return these initial phone calls as soon as possible. Since L.A. has about a million therapists, it is likely that the patient has already called a few other people. Although it doesn't make a great deal of sense, patients often choose the therapist who returns their call first and can schedule them for an appointment right away. I tried this strategy once for having my car detailed and I am happy to report that the technique works great.

Some patients are truly "therapist shopping." They actually let you know that they have had, or have scheduled, an appointment with one or two other therapists. On the surface this seems like a reasonable approach. My ten a.m. patient today is therapist shopping. After doing my best to convince him of my competence, the patient asks me how he can decide between seeing me and seeing the other therapist he has already seen. My first inclination is to simply tell him he would be making the biggest mistake of his life if he didn't see me. However, I refrain from doing this and tell him how he can't go wrong with either of us. In this case I actually know the other therapist and don't really believe the statement but I think that this comment will score extra points and swing the decision in my favor. He decides to schedule another appointment with me. I feel like I just hit a home run.

November 25

I have seven patients scheduled for today. At noon I have a new patient who has a mild case of OCD. After telling her about the treatment options she decides that she wants to get a referral for medication. This is in spite of the fact that I explained to her that medications are not as effective as behavioral therapy for OCD. I informed her that the relapse rate is very high if she goes off medications and she has had no other treatment for her OCD. Since psychologists cannot prescribe medications in California, it is necessary for me to refer patients to psychiatrists who will prescribe them. Since I have been in practice for so long I know many psychiatrists in the L.A. area. Just like any profession there is a wide range of competence in practicing psychiatrists. Confession number thirty-one: I basically have two criteria for giving out a referral to a psychiatrist. First, the psychiatrist must be competent in my eyes. Secondly, the psychiatrist needs to refer patients to me. Most of the psychiatrists I refer to could also be called psychopharmacologists. They do some psychotherapy, but it is generally limited and does not usually include cognitive behavioral therapy. So, when psychiatrists have patients who could benefit from cognitive behavioral therapy they generally refer the patient to other therapists. If I continually refer patients to psychiatrist X and he never refers patients back to me, I have to assume he is (1) referring to other therapists, (2) doesn't think I am competent, (3) has had bad reports about me from previous patients he has sent to me, or (4) doesn't believe in the efficacy of cognitive behavioral therapy. I believe these reasons to be accurate, because they are basically the same reasons I would not refer a patient to a psychiatrist. None of the reasons are appealing if you are not getting back referrals from someone you refer to.

One reason I won't refer to a particular psychiatrist who I think is competent is when I get negative reports back from patients. If these reports are accurate, and I believe some of them are, it is amazing to me the way some people run their practices. One patient told me that his psychiatrist would not allow profanity in the session. This might work well in church, but many therapy patients swear like truckers. Many psychiatrists do not return calls within a reasonable time. If I were a patient who had questions about a medication I was given, I would be especially concerned about this. In calling many psychiatry offices you have to deal with a secretary who basically functions as a roadblock to your speaking directly to the psychiatrist. Some psychiatrists never get back to the referring person to give them feedback about the patient. To all psychiatrists who might read this book: Please rehearse and learn the following phrase: "Thank you for referring Joe Patient to me." I was always taught to at least say thank you when someone does something nice for you. I am actually giving the psychiatrist business. I do not think that a thank you is too much to ask. There is one psychiatrist who I refer patients to, and who also refers me patients, who sends a box of chocolates to me every Christmas.

November 26

It is the day before the start of five days off because of the Thanksgiving holiday. This fact puts me in a good mood to start the day. It does not take long for that mood to change. While seeing my one o'clock patient my pager goes off. I carry a pager for emergencies but patients know that it may take up to forty-five minutes for me to return a page if I am in session with another patient. I never interrupt the session to return a page but I often look at the pager to see who is calling. When I look this time I recognize the number of an old patient who has paged me many times before. I press the button on the pager so it will stop chirping. After about another minute the pager goes off again and reads "duplicate." I again turn the pager off, apologize to the patient, and resume therapy. The pager appears to go off approximately ten times in a row and I keep turning it off. I decide to just turn the pager to vibrate and put it on my desk. A few minutes later the pager starts to vibrate and move across my desk. I turn it off and a minute later it does the same thing. Now I am thoroughly pissed at this patient, but it is difficult for me to not laugh at the pager moving across the desk. I decide to hold the pager in my hand for the remainder of the session. Each time it goes off I try to press the button to make it stop without losing concentration on the therapy session. At the end of the session, I profusely apologize to the patient in my office and then I return the page. After talking to the patient for a few minutes I decide to very politely tell him that he did not need to page me thirty-seven times. He told me I was exaggerating, but I don't think I really was.

I probably get paged about once a week and most of the calls are legitimate clinical emergencies. If someone is suicidal or in the midst of a horrible panic attack I don't mind returning the page. Confession number thirty-two: I hate returning pages during movies or in the middle of the night. If I return a page during a movie I am going to miss a significant amount of the movie and then I have to go back into the theatre and watch the end of the movie. Most of the time I am not very alert and focused when I return pages at three a.m. For every legitimate page there are probably two absurd pages. What constitutes an inappropriate page? If you are a therapy patient here are some rules for paging a therapist. (1) Do not page your therapist if you have never had a session with him. (2) Do not page your therapist to make or change an appointment. (3) Do not page your therapist to ask him a question that he has answered 5000 times before. (4) Do not page your therapist if you haven't paid your bill for the past three months. (5) Do not page your therapist and put in a return work number that is not your individual extension. I have had times when I return a page and a receptionist for a company answers the phone. "Yes, this is Dr. Tarlow. Did any of the 2000 employees in your firm page me?" (6) Do not page your therapist and put in the wrong return phone number. (7) Do not page your therapist after canceling your last few appointments and now you need to talk to him immediately. (8) Do not page your therapist and expect a full therapy session on the phone. And, perhaps the most important paging rule: (9) do not page your therapist and then not be at the return phone number when your therapist calls back. This last problem has occurred very frequently for me. A patient pages me, I finish my session, I return the page and I get an answering machine. I guess it was such an emergency that the patient could not stick around and wait for my return call.

My pager has actually become a part of me. Except for vacations I take it everywhere. I think someday I may have to have it surgically removed from my body.

CHAPTER 3
December

December 2

My three o'clock patient, NV, is another good patient. NV had a serious depression and was actually hospitalized for it just prior to his coming to me for therapy. For many of my patients I assign a self help book to be used in conjunction with the therapy. The term "self-help" is really a misnomer. George Carlin once said if you are following someone else's suggestions how could that be self-help? There are actually some wonderful psychology self- help books. Confession number thirty-three: If all patients could read the best self-help books and follow the exercises in the book they probably would put most therapists out of business. However, most patients can't follow the exercises in the book on their own, and they need someone to guide them through the process. There is one other small problem. If you go into a bookstore you will find about three thousand self-help books in the psychology section. Now, it is nice to have such a wide choice, but if you know very little about psychology how do you pick one out? I am sure if you read the testimonials on the book cover it would lead you to believe that the book is the definitive work on the problem you have. I think every therapist wants to write a self-help book.

About ten years ago a patient I was treating for fear of flying came into the session and asked me what I thought of the book *The Five Minute Phobia Cure*. Since I had never heard of the book I couldn't give the patient my opinion and she volunteered to bring me her copy of the book. I think I did have a slight prejudice in reading the book towards trying to ensure that was a scam. Just imagine a psychologist who has discovered a technique that can cure a patient of their phobia in five minutes. This would essentially put me out of business. As it turns out the "cure" involved touching patients in a certain way. The author included many case histories, but no good research studies. Lucky for me; I was still in business.

NV is very motivated to get better. He always reads the assigned chapter in the book and then comes into the session with all his homework completed. However, he is often confused by the book and needs me to clarify many of the points in it. This clarification generally takes the entire session. Since I probably haven't read the book myself in over five years I have to be able to improvise my responses.

Many patients never complete their homework assignments from the book. I often feel like a high school teacher listening to the excuses for why the homework was not completed. "Dr. Tarlow, I couldn't fill in that chart because I left it in my car which was stolen. When I got the car back the only thing missing was the chart."

December 3

I have six patients scheduled for today. My four p.m. patient is an initial evaluation for the UCLA OCD program. Before people are admitted to the program they must come to me for a one-hour evaluation. Most of these patients already know they have severe OCD. They have often been in treatment for months or years prior to seeing me. Almost all of them have not improved in their previous treatment or they wouldn't be seeing me now. I do see a wide range of severity of OCD during these interviews. Some people just have mild symptoms that really do not necessitate the UCLA program, and other people have such severe symptoms that it is amazing they were able to make it to the interview. The most severe OCD patient I ever saw was a man who entered my office wearing seven pairs of surgical gloves. After touching anything in my office he would take off a pair of the gloves and throw them away. He stood in the middle of my office the entire session, not able to sit on my furniture. He was so anxious during the session that his teeth were chattering as if he was in sub-freezing weather without a coat. Most OCD patients are not this severe.

My favorite OCD symptom of all time is the patient who had to eat all of her food in alphabetical order. Each time she would have a meal, she would arrange the food on her plate in alphabetical order and then eat it in that order. For example, apples, bread, chicken and then potato.

Most of the OCD patients do fairly well in treatment and get better. As I mentioned previously the major treatment for these patients is actually to expose them to their fears. It is my job to design these "assignments" for the patient. Some of these assignments are rather simple to devise. For example, for the patient who ate her food in alphabetical order the assignment was to simply eat her food randomly. After doing this for a few days the patient no longer is concerned with the order of her food. There have actually been very few times that these assignments backfire. One that does come to mind is the time that I was treating a fairly famous actor. He told me that he had to turn around five times in the shower to prevent bad things from happening to himself or his family. Now, you don't have to be a psychologist to realize that the assignment I asked him to complete was to take a shower without turning around. After successfully following that assignment for three days an article appeared in the LA Times critiquing every movie this patient had made. It was a scathing, unflattering article describing this person as one of the worst actors ever. He came to the next session, threw the article at me and said, "You asked me to stop my ritual and look what happened." He left the session and never returned again.

One of my rules of OCD treatment is to never ask anyone to do anything I couldn't do. There are some patients I ask to do some outrageous things. If a patient has an obsession about contamination, I may ask him to stick his hands in a trash can and then lick his fingers. If a patient has an obsession about her house burning down, I may ask her to leave the oven on all day when she leaves her house. Patients often ask me if the "bad" thing ever happens. I tell them I have lots of malpractice insurance.

In my supervision of other therapists, I try to get them to apply the same rules about giving assignments to patients. However, I have found that many therapists do not like to take as many risks as I do. Interestingly, the most controversial exposure assignment seems to be in the use of public restrooms. Many therapists I have supervised have told me that they have to use the protective liners to be able to sit on the toilet seat. I think this is a touch of OCD. After giving patients many of these assignments they often think I am some extreme risk taker. The patients generally stop asking me if I would do the assignment but they want to know if people who do not have OCD would do the assignment. To help motivate them I place a call to a "random" friend and ask the friend over the speakerphone if they would do the assignment. Confession number thirty-four: this is a setup. I have told this person to always answer yes. No matter what question I ask my friend she always answers yes. "Would you sit on a toilet in a public restroom without a toilet seat cover?" "Yes." "Would you leave the oven on all day?" "Yes." Would you drive down Wilshire Boulevard with your eyes closed?" "Yes!" I often enjoy calling the person back and asking if she would really do what I asked.

December 5

I learned today that one of my patients has a serious drinking problem. Although I am not an expert on substance abuse I am required by the licensing board to have some knowledge in that area. I am not required to treat the person for his problem. However, I need to make a referral to some sort of treatment program. The first program that always comes to mind is AA (Alcoholics Anonymous). There are definitely some wonderful aspects to the AA program but I have some difficulty with a few of their steps. Confession number thirty-five: I cannot in good conscience tell patients to admit they are powerless over their problem. The whole basis of the type of therapy that I practice is self-control. I want the patient to learn that they can control their problems. If I took this AA philosophy to an extreme, I would have to tell patients that they could not control their fears, their panic attacks, their compulsions or their mood in general. I do not find the AA philosophy works for every patient. However, it seems like the philosophy is expanding. Every time I check there is a new spin-off on AA. Marijuana Anonymous, Cocaine Anonymous, Overeaters Anonymous, Sex Addicts Anonymous, Clutterers Anonymous, etc. I expect to see Pro Football Watchers Anonymous, Spending Too Much

Time with My Dog Anonymous and People Who Are Addicted to Seeing Their Therapists Anonymous in the near future.

There is an alternative program called "moderation management" that believes some people with drinking problems are capable of social drinking. This is pure heresy to people who believe in AA. However, the philosophy of the program fits better into to my belief system.

December 6

I had three patients today who actually ran out of things to say. The concept of a forty-five to fifty minute therapy session is actually quite arbitrary. I would like to be able to charge by the minute and end the session whenever both the patient and I have run out of therapeutic conversation. However, this would leave some significant gaps in my schedule where I would have no one in my office.

All three of today's patients actually had completed their therapeutic assignments and were given assignments for next week by about ten to fifteen minutes into the therapy. The first patient then chose to discuss movies with me. Confession number thirty-six: Getting paid to discuss movies turns out to be an enjoyable way to make a living. I wonder if going to the movies could actually be considered continuing education for my license renewal.

The next patient wanted to discuss pro basketball. I feel I must really be in heaven. Getting paid to discuss one of my favorite things in the world. Is this what a sports talk show host feels like?

The third patient decided he had nothing he wanted to talk to me about and told me he would pay for the session and just leave early. I don't try too hard to discourage this behavior. Some patients require a bouncer to get them out of the office and others don't really want to be there in the first place.

December 9

I believe that most of my patients like me. I actually work hard at being likeable. Returning phone calls promptly, being on time, and being empathic are just some of the likeable qualities I strive for. Every now and then I run into a patient that I don't get along with. Today I didn't just run into one, I collided with one of these patients. My two p.m. patient was a new patient referred by another psychologist. I ask new patients to come to the first session about ten minutes early to fill out the new patient registration form and consent for treatment form. Upon greeting this new patient and handing her the forms, she informed me that she wasn't filling out any forms or signing any consent for treatment. My initial thought is to say, "Get out of my office." However, my years of experience and my fear of being sued by patients prevent me from saying that. The patient is clearly paranoid. I run the Center for Anxiety Management, not the Center for Paranoid Disorders. So, I am not used to dealing with this kind of patient. I convince her to come into my office and I try to calm her down. I then try to figure out how I can help her but she just doesn't like the fact that I am asking her a lot of questions. After about ten minutes of questioning she gets frustrated and wants to know how I can help her. I try to convince her that I need to know her diagnosis before I can treat her. She doesn't buy this line of reasoning, becomes more agitated, and walks out of my office. Confession number thirty-seven: there are times that I am glad certain patients quit. I don't even care about charging her for the session. All I care about is that she never comes back to see me.

My favorite story about a patient quitting therapy occurred last year. This patient, let's call her SH, had an eight a.m. appointment with me. She left a message a few minutes before the appointment telling me that she was having a panic attack and could not make the appointment. As soon as I received the message I called the patient at her home to help calm her down. However, she either was not home or did not answer the phone. I left a message telling SH that I would be happy to talk to her on the phone instead of her coming in for the session. SH asked me to call her after nine p.m. at her home. I talked to her for about thirty minutes on the phone later that night. The next week SH showed up for her appointment. At the end of the session I informed her that I would not be charging her for the missed appointment, but if it happened again that I would charge her. I then expected to hear a big "thank you." I was not prepared for what she actually said. SH became very belligerent and told me I had violated the principle of doing no harm to the patient and that she would not be returning to therapy. Imagine what would have happened if I actually had charged her for the session as was indicated in my office policy.

December 9

Every Tuesday at one p.m. I have a supervision session with one of my psychological assistants. A psychological assistant is a person in the process of obtaining supervised hours in order to be able to take the licensing exam. I usually supply the assistant with patients, office space, and supervision of the cases. In exchange, the psychological assistants give me fifty percent of the income they collect. Every psychologist who has been in practice for three years is allowed to supervise up to three psychological assistants. I try to refer the patients who cannot afford to see me to my psychological assistants. The more patients these assistants see, the more money I make. This is actually a very sweet setup when you have someone working for you who is honest, competent, and wants to see a lot of patients. After the first few months of supervision, I generally realize that these people require very little supervision.

During supervision my psychological assistants generally review all of the cases they are seeing. I am expected to make sure the patient is receiving good treatment and that the psychological assistant is abiding by all of the ethical standards and California laws governing the practice of therapy. Some of these regulations seem to have been written by people who know very little about psychotherapy. Here are a few of my favorites: Supervision must consist of one hour of face-to-face supervision for every ten patient hours. If my math were correct that would mean six minutes per patient per week. This also means that I can't do supervision on the phone. I often do my supervision during lunch, and I try to look at the psychological assistant while I am eating in order to make sure I am satisfying the face-to-face supervision requirement.

Another interesting regulation is that the psychological assistant's supervisor must be on the premises at least fifty percent of the time the psychological assistant is seeing patients. Let me try to understand the logic of this rule. Fifty percent of the time I assume the psychological assistant will need me during the course of her sessions and the other fifty percent of the time I can be at Disneyland. Confession number thirty-eight: I know some psychologists who are around only forty-eight percent of the time. What do the psychologists in private practice do who share an office with their psychological assistant? Do they wait in the waiting room while the psychological assistant is seeing his patients?

One of the questions I often get from new patients who cannot afford my fee is whether the psychological assistant is as good as I am. This question ranks somewhere in the top ten stupid questions of all time. What do these people really expect me to say? "Well, I have been doing this for over thirty years and my psychological assistant has been practicing for nine months and is far and away better than I." What I would like to say is, "You get what you pay for."

I have generally been very pleased with the psychological assistants I have chosen. There was one exception about ten years ago. I hired one person who I am quite sure was stealing my patients. You may wonder how a patient can be stolen. The psychological assistant was answering the phones and scheduling new patients for him. He would then tell me during supervision that he had a new patient who had contacted him directly. I often wanted to have a friend call and pretend to be a new patient and see what he would do. Despite my best private detective skills, I was never able to catch him doing anything unethical or illegal. I guess that makes him a good psychopath.

December 12

As it gets closer to the holidays I seem to get more and more cancellations. As long as I can pay my bills these cancellations make me happy. One of the other things that happen around the holidays is that some patients give me presents. The general rule is that I am not supposed to accept gifts from patients. Confession number thirty-nine: I have accepted some gifts from patients. I don't always keep the gift. Most of the time the gifts are so small and personal that it would just feel wrong not to accept them. Today one patient gave me some homemade cookies. Since I am sure that this patient thinks highly of me, I will eat the cookies. There have been times where I have thrown out cookies and cakes given to me by certain patients. This occurred more often after I heard the following story: A psychologist was given a cake by one of his patients. He was trying to decide whether to eat the cake, take it home to his family, or leave it in the waiting room. He finally decided just to throw it out. When the patient returned for the next session he asked the psychologist if he liked the cake. The psychologist lied and said it was good. The patient then told the psychologist that he had ejaculated into the cake batter.

Several years ago one patient gave me some cookies from his homeland. I will not name the country to avoid tons of potential hate mail. He asked me to try one of the cookies in the session. The cookies turned out to be one of the vilest tasting foods I had ever eaten. I ate the cookie, put on a fake smile and told the patient how delicious they were. I felt like a mother trying to make her child feel good about his first attempt at cooking. At the end of the session I threw out the rest of the cookies.

Other presents I have received included plants, bottles of wine and photographs the patient has taken. Most of these gifts are very thoughtful. It does seem that these gifts put me on the same level as the patient's hairdresser.

December 13

I go to see the movie "Analyze That" tonight. I always am interested in how therapists are portrayed in movies. I am also interested in how patient problems are displayed in the movie. The first problem I have with the movie is that Billy Crystal is the spitting image of a psychiatrist friend of mine. I have a hard time watching the movie without thinking what is Michael Gitlin doing in this movie? One of the scenes takes place in the therapist's house where he has an office. There are some therapists who see patients in their house, but not many. In the movie the character played by Robert DiNiro is released from prison into the custody of the therapist, Billy Crystal. To live with your patient 24/7 would essentially be every therapist's nightmare.

I actually know of two colleagues who see patients in their house. Confession number forty: I don't want patients to know my address, let alone see my house. I can't imagine letting a patient in my front door and telling him to just step over my son's toys on the way to the office. I can't imagine being interrupted by the housekeeper asking me what drawer to put my wife's thong in. Therapists with an office in their home often have a separate entrance and therefore don't have to deal with these problems.

December 16

It is the first really bad weather day in L.A. in some time. It has been pouring most of the day and the traffic is horrendous. Many people in L.A. do not know how to drive in the rain. This drastically affects my practice. No one is on time and some patients miss their entire appointment because of being stuck in traffic. I don't mind having the short sessions and being paid for an entire session. I try to understand about being stuck in traffic and often do not charge patients who really have tried to get to the appointment.

One of my patients today is British. This presents a small problem for me since I apparently do not speak the same language as she does. She actually used two words today that I had never heard. The first was "whank" and the second was "smegma." Confession number forty-one: Most of the time I pretend that I know every vocabulary word known to man. Today I was feeling particularly assertive and actually asked the patient what these words meant. The patient informed me that "whank" means penis and "smegma" means the material that is left under the foreskin of an uncircumcised male. I am not happy that I asked her.

December 17

The central theme of several sessions today was stress management. It sometimes amazes me that people are so innately poor at handling stress. "Doc, I'm working eighty hours per week and feel totally stressed out. What should I do?" Why does it seem the majority of stress-management cases are attorneys? It would be so much easier if the law schools only admitted anyone who wanted to work more than sixty hours per week.

A few years ago a patient came to my office and told me that he had a sleep problem. He informed me that he was sleeping six hours per night and wanted to learn to sleep just four hours per night. He reasoned that since he didn't accomplish anything when he was sleeping, that the time was wasted.

Confession number forty-two: Since I hardly ever feel very stressed I try to get patients to adapt many of my habits in order to deal better with stress. I preach the importance of exercise, vacation time, and time management. Then I tell them that I will be away on vacation next week.

December 19

Many people have asked me if I get bored with hearing patient's talk about the same problems every day. I tell them that every time I think I have heard it all it seems like I am presented with a new problem that I have never heard before. Today was one of those days. I'm sure you remember my patient who was concerned about how she was poking her ear too frequently while she slept. She informed me today that several doctors have told her that she produces an incredible amount of earwax. We spend a significant amount of the session talking about earwax. It is a first for me. No one in all my years of practice has ever talked to me about earwax. Confession number forty-three: I am afraid to tell her that I use Q-tips every day and have never had a problem with earwax. I also have a secret desire to ask her if her husband ever sticks his tongue in her ears and what is his reaction afterwards. Again, my therapeutic judgment prevails and I am very serious for the entire session. I know that many of my patients who read this book will have trouble identifying themselves as the patients I am talking about. I have a suspicion that this patient may know I was talking about her.

My first patient of the day is a new referral from a friend of mine who is a psychologist. There are certain reasons one psychologist might refer to another psychologist. (1) If the psychologist is completely booked and can't convince the patient to wait for an opening. (2) If the psychologist really believes that a different psychologist is more of an expert in a particular area. And (3) if the psychologist believes that the patient could benefit from a different orientation. In this case, none of these reasons apply. This patient wants a therapist who has an office near where she lives. She had already made an appointment with another therapist but cancelled the appointment when she found out my office was closer. I wonder if I set up therapy outlets at all 7-11's if my business would boom. This patient never asked me about my experience, my therapeutic orientation, or even what I charged. Since my basic assumption is that there are thousands of incompetent therapists in L.A., this patient was at least lucky to find me. After meeting with her she decides to continue in therapy with me.

December 20

It is my last day before a week's vacation. Most of my vacations over the past twenty years have been for only a week. It gives me just enough time to relax and prepare for any problems my patients present. I believe many therapists fear that if they went away for three weeks that their patients would soon discover that they did not really need the therapist and the therapist would return to work with thirty messages canceling all of the next week's appointments. Confession number forty-four: It is always good to see your therapist the day before the therapist's vacation. The therapist should be in a very good mood.

I also received a new referral today from a fairly famous psychiatrist. It makes me feel pretty good that this person has faith in me as a therapist. The patient's problem is compulsive shopping. Since I have seen hundreds of OCD patients many people assume that I can treat any problem that is compulsive in nature. Compulsive eating, compulsive exercising, compulsive gambling, compulsive stealing, compulsive sex, compulsive ear poking, compulsive working, compulsive scratching, compulsive hair pulling, compulsive nail biting, compulsive anything. Please keep in mind that just because a behavior occurs compulsively it does not mean that the patient has OCD. If the behavior gives the patient pleasure than it is not OCD.

Compulsive shopping is certainly an interesting problem. Confession number forty-five: If everyone in L.A. were successfully treated for compulsive shopping it would probably bankrupt half of the businesses in Beverly Hills. I will probably see this new patient but, as with many non-OCD compulsions, it is unadvisable to completely eliminate the behavior. I sometimes imagine the patient's wife coming to see me at the end of therapy. "Dr. Tarlow, my husband appears completely cured of his compulsive shopping. The only problem is that he won't buy anything anymore."

December 21

It is officially the first day of my vacation. I am flying to Vancouver to go skiing with my family for one week. No patients, no pagers, no mail, no phone calls. Wrong!! On the plane I get to sit next to a woman who has a fear of flying. She asks me if I have any fear of flying. Now, I could just tell her no and leave it at that or tell her what I do and provide her with a free therapy session. I guess there is a little altruism within me. I decide to try to help her after she takes one Xanax and two scotch and sodas. I get her to change some of her thoughts about the dangers of flying. I get her to relax. The only thing I can't get her to do is to believe that the only reason the plane landed safely was because of God and the two angel pins she was wearing. I didn't want to tell her about the fear of flying patient I treated a few years ago. I was treating this patient through the "flooding" technique. This involved taking six flights in one day. Prior to the first flight the patient told me that she had to pray to God that the flight would take off and land safely. I convinced her that we would both pray as hard as we could that the plane would crash. Since I am writing about this now you can assume that our prayers did not come true.

One of the problems with using flooding with fear of flying is that you often run into the same crew when you take a flight that immediately returns to the city where you started. There was one time when no matter what I said the flight attendant would not believe that I didn't work for the airline and was there to evaluate the crew. They did treat me very nicely on that flight.

December 30

Another first day back from vacation. However, many of my patients are away on vacation so that I actually have a lighter day than usual. First thing I do is to return all of my calls from the previous week. It is amazing to me how many people do not listen to my outgoing message on my answering machine. The message clearly stated that I was out of town and would not return until December 29. Several people left messages saying they had called me earlier in the week and I hadn't returned their phone calls.

The next task is to open my mail from the previous week. I try to open all the checks first. It is very reinforcing to have a number of checks waiting for you after you haven't worked for a week. It takes a while to find all of the checks interspersed within the psychological junk mail: notices of new books, conference announcements, continuing education classes and waiting room magazines.

Confession number forty-six: It gets harder and harder to return to work after vacations. A friend asked me if I was ready to go back to work today. I told him that I had not been ready to go back to work for the past seven years. Maybe I'm just not in therapy shape. You know how in order to run a marathon you have to train for a long time. Maybe I have neglected my therapy training. I really didn't have to listen to anyone the past week while I was skiing. I hardly had to answer any questions. I didn't have to have good eye contact. I didn't need to be empathic. For the most part I didn't have to use my brain very much. Maybe I need to practice these skills the day before I return to work after a vacation.

The first four patients are fairly difficult and draining. However, the fifth patient is actually fun because she has a sense of humor. She is the only patient who I have told that I am writing this book. I really wanted to tape her session today but she did not give me permission. She also informed me that she was not going to be entertaining today. Well, that was just wrong. It was a very entertaining session as she told me about how she ended an affair with a married man by deciding to tell his wife that she was having an affair with her husband for the past six months. If this type of story is not entertaining, I don't know what is.

December 31

I was scheduled to be on jury duty this week. I have never had to serve on a jury before. In past years each time a summons for jury duty arrived I would ask to be excused because I had suicidal patients and needed to be on call twenty-four hours per day. Confession number forty-seven: This is not the real reason I wanted to be excused. If I serve on a jury, which I do believe is an important function; I will get paid five dollars per day. Essentially, I will have a week without any income. It seems unfair that people who are in private practice have the same responsibility regarding jury duty as someone who works for a company that pays him while he is on jury duty. However, I did think about which week I would be the least hurt financially and which week I would be the least likely to end up on a jury and I concluded it would be the last week of the year. I assumed even judges and attorneys take some time off. So far my thinking has been correct. I was not needed on Monday or Tuesday and Wednesday is a holiday. The most days I will have to serve are two. I do occasionally get this bad dream that I have been chosen to be on a jury for a murder trial. The trial lasts three months during which time I am sequestered and unable to watch NBA basketball games.

Since it is the last day of the year I try to think about the previous year and what I have accomplished. Many of the last seven or eight years are very similar. I see private patients and work at the UCLA OCD program. I don't think my "cure" rate was any better this year than any of the previous seven years. I know an athlete can generally tell when they have reached their peak in terms of performance. I wonder if I have peaked therapeutically. I wonder if my "cure" rate may even start to go down. How do you know when to retire from psychotherapy? When I decide to retire, do I hold a press conference and tell the world, "I wanted to go out on top. There are too many therapists who practice way past their prime. I want my patients to remember me the way I am now."

Sometimes something not happening can be looked at as a positive thing. I didn't get sued for malpractice this year, although a few patients did threaten.

I do think I have become a little better known in the field of anxiety disorders and cognitive behavioral treatment. It sometimes amazes me that people who I think I have never met say they know me. Then again, this may just be my own memory problem.

It was another very successful financial year. I think I have become very good at running my practice as a business. I am not sure I can make any more money than I have this year; especially if I start to cut down on the number of patients I see every week.

Finally, starting this book is something I feel very good about. It has really helped me in maintaining my focus and my desire to continue to see patients.

CHAPTER 4
January

January 2

The start of a new year means patients who actually have New Year's resolutions. I think there is actually research on New Year's resolutions indicating that the majority of them do not last a month. Confession number forty-eight: I also make resolutions. This year I resolve to; (1) finish this book, (2) obtain my promotion at UCLA from associate to full professor, (3) cut down on the number of patients I see each week, (4) develop new ways to earn passive income, and (5) lose fifteen pounds (doesn't everyone have this one?).

January 3

I had another new patient today. This fifty year old man had been in therapy most of his adult life for anxiety. He told me about two of the therapists that he had seen who were not able to help him. One of them, a psychoanalyst who he saw for eight years, five days a week. I believe that is financially equivalent to the price of an average house. If the average fee per session was $150 (a low estimate) and you multiply that times fifty-two weeks times five days per week times eight years you get $312,000. Confession number forty-nine: there are times that I wouldn't mind being an analyst. If I could find three patients I really liked and could see them every day and charge $225 per session I would be able to work three hours a day and earn $209,250 a year.

Another bonus you get with psychoanalytic patients is that you never have to worry about the patient getting better and stopping therapy.

This patient also saw another therapist for thirteen years. When I asked if this therapist had helped him the patient replied, "She couldn't help me; she was a drunk." Did it really take this patient thirteen years to figure out that he should quit therapy with this therapist? If I can teach this patient one thing it will be that if he doesn't like me or isn't getting better that he can quit therapy within the first few months.

Some therapists actually make their patients feel guilty for quitting therapy. I am sure I could probably convince ninety percent of my patients to continue in therapy and work on other issues. However, it often is very empowering for patients to realize that they have overcome a problem and are ready to stop treatment.

January 6

My ten a.m. patient is slightly paranoid. She is concerned that she may give someone a dirty look and that person will follow her home and hurt her or her family. I have two big picture windows in my office. They look out on trees and a parking lot. Each time this patient enters my office says that there is too much glare coming through the windows and asks whether I would mind if she closes the blinds? This same thing happens every week for a few months. In the summer it does get somewhat bright in the office. However, this is January and it is a dark and cloudy day. It only took me a few months to figure out that what she really wanted was not to be seen in my office. I have to decide when a good time to confront her is. I suspect that she will deny that this is the true reason she is shutting the blinds. I am considering just removing the blinds and telling her they are being repaired to see what she does. My guess is she would then sit with her back to the window. My other choice was to ask her to go over to the window and purposely give people in the parking lot dirty looks. I try practicing this in the mirror and find that is hard to give dirty looks if you are not really upset at someone. It is easier to just use your middle finger.

This patient also pays me cash for each session. It is likely that she wants no record of being seen by a psychologist. This is somewhat common and I have had many other patients do this over the past thirty years. Confession number fifty: I sometimes imagine I am a psychopath and I am going to blackmail all of these patients. I send them a blackmail note stating: "Put $10,000 in unmarked bills in an envelope and put it in the dumpster and no one will ever know that you have been in therapy." Some patients actually ask if it is okay if they pay in cash. Has anyone ever turned down a cash payment?

It amazes me how many people are, or have been, in therapy and yet it is still so unacceptable to many people. I had a patient a few years ago who applied to graduate school and put in his application essay that he had bipolar disorder and was in therapy. I know this person was more qualified for this school than most of the students who are accepted. However, he was rejected and we both hypothesized that the reason was the essay. He applied again the next year, excluding the information from the essay and was accepted. What makes this story very interesting is that the graduate program he entered was in clinical psychology. If a clinical psychology graduate program has a problem with a person having a psychiatric diagnosis, and being in therapy, then my patients are probably correct in trying to hide that information.

January 7

I had to make a house call today. Believe it or not, some psychologists will do that. I am usually happy to make house calls because it allows me to get out of the office and I actually get paid for my travel time by the patient. There are generally only two types of patients for whom I would make house calls. The first are agoraphobic patients who are unable to leave their house because of the fear of having a panic attack. The second are OCD patients whose specific problems require my working with them in their home environment. Many of the OCD patients, including the one today, are "hoarders." Hoarders tend to save things that are not valuable. They have difficulty throwing anything away. Today's patient is one of the worst hoarders I have ever seen. It is difficult to even move around in her apartment because of the stacks of paper piled everywhere. Her bed, kitchen, and living room are essentially unusable because of the clutter. There is a funny odor in the apartment. I would not be surprised to find a dead animal at the bottom of one her piles.

Part of my job when working with hoarders is to teach them how to throw things away and how to organize everything else. We start with a pile of old newspapers and junk mail on her kitchen table. The patient is afraid to throw away a great deal of the junk mail because of the potential money saving coupons that are present. The only problem with this strategy is that the coupons expired months ago. After digging through to the bottom of one pile of papers we discover rat droppings. Confession number fifty-one: I want to run out of this house as fast as I can. If there are rat droppings there, could the rats be far behind? I manage to help her throw away a lot of old newspapers. I am sure many people could be trained very quickly to do this aspect of my job. All you have to do is look at the patient and repeat the following line: "Throw it away." For some patients who continue to stare at the hoarded items, it is necessary to repeat the same line several times.

This patient also has a refrigerator in her kitchen that is plugged in but she has not been able to open it for twenty-two years because of the papers piled up in front of the refrigerator door. I have had some very bad dreams about the food that we would find in there when the refrigerator is finally opened. I would guess I would not have to look at the expiration date on the milk to determine if it should be thrown away.

There are some things even hoarders should save. However, most of them are so unorganized that there is no logical place to put these things. One of the dilemmas in treating hoarders is that if you start a file of something that should be saved, where do you put the file? Watching some of these patients try to find something in their house is quite amusing. Now where did I put that paper with the important phone number on it?

January 8

Today is my birthday and I have no patients scheduled. I think from now on I will always plan to not work on my birthday. Now if I can only get someone to cover for me so I won't have to wear my pager.

January 9

Another reason I sometimes leave my office for a patient is to help a patient overcome a fear. One of the most common phobias in L.A. is a fear of driving on the freeway. I often drive with patients to help them overcome this fear. Today I was seeing a patient that I had seen once before for a driving phobia. The first session was an in office session where I determined that this patient did have a driving phobia and the patient agreed to be treated with behavioral therapy. I told the patient that I needed to see her drive before we started any of the behavioral treatment. I asked her to meet me in front of the office the following week and I would evaluate her phobia and her driving skills. I would say that ninety-nine percent of the patients I have seen for driving phobia have actually been very good drivers. Not this patient! After getting on the freeway the patient was only able to go forty-five MPH and stay in the right lane. When you travel that slowly on the LA freeways you immediately notice gigantic trucks in your rear view mirror that appear to be in your back seat. If you didn't have anxiety before, you sure do now. After taking time for a short prayer, I asked the patient to exit the freeway. I thought I would have her drive on a winding city street. However, while driving on this winding road, the patient informed me that she sometimes "blacks out" on similar roads. After a more lengthy prayer, I asked her to tell me if she thought that she was about to black out. About ten minutes later the patient closed her eyes briefly. I raised my voice to get her to open her eyes and told her to drive back to my office. Upon returning to my office I advised her to come back to see me after about eight years of driving lessons.

Some patients have told me that I was very brave to be driving in the car with them. I informed them that I had a big life insurance policy. Most of the driving patients do quite well in these sessions. Confession number fifty-three: It again feels strange to be getting paid for simply riding in a car with a patient and every few minutes saying, "You are doing great!" Many of these patients are afraid to go fast on the freeway. This is getting to be less and less of a problem in L.A. since there is generally no time of the day when you can go fast.

January 10

As I let one of my patients into my office today, she informed me that there is nothing good to read in my waiting room. I probably subscribe to ten different magazines just for the waiting room. I try to have a variety of sports, travel, business, news, fitness, and gossip-type magazines. It appears she did not like my taste in magazines. She felt there should be poetry and literature available in the waiting room. I wonder if she thought my therapy office doubled as the local library. I gently informed her that it is not against the rules of therapy to bring her own book to read in the waiting room. Another patient today told me that he must be getting old because when he was looking at the magazines in the waiting room, he picked up the one with the BMW on the cover and not the one with the supermodel.

I swore when I went into private practice that I would always keep current issues of magazines in my waiting room. I have been in other doctor's offices during the last year and I recall picking up an issue of Newsweek and discovering that we are in the middle of a war with Vietnam. I have seen some outstanding collections of National Geographic from the 1980s. I promised myself I would throw out any issues of magazines more than two months old.

Confession number fifty-four: Patients steal magazines. Certain magazines usually disappear quicker. After an unscientific study I recently conducted at my office I found that the three magazines that disappear the quickest are: (1) *TV Guide*, (2) *Sports Illustrated* and (3) *People*. *TV Guide* never lasts past the first day that it is put in the waiting room. The following magazines never seem to disappear: (1) *Readers Digest*, (2) *Discover* and (3) *Newsweek*. I thought about having a hidden camera in the waiting room just to see how careful patients are in not allowing anyone to see them stealing the magazine. It would also be interesting therapeutic material for a session in case the patient did not have much to talk about. I wonder if some patients think the magazines are included in their fee.

January 13

The problem of the day centers on how to motivate patients to complete therapeutic homework assignments. I have three patients today who are not very motivated to do so. The first person has a goal of completing her homework for a class she is taking. The next person has to practice taking elevators three times per week. The final person needs to complete her math assignments in school. I happen to be a big believer in both reinforcement and punishment principles. I believe it is possible to motivate most people with the correct combination of rewards and punishment. I ask each of the patients the same question: "If I were to give you $20,000 if you completed your assignment by the next session, would you do it?" As usual every patient tells me that they would complete their assignment for $20,000. I then inform them that my wife has stopped me from offering this incentive and we have to arrive at a different reward. As much as I believe in the power of rewards, it appears that too many of my patients have difficulty figuring out what reward they could get that they are not already getting. So, it is with great regret that I turn to that other form of motivation - punishment. People tend to be especially motivated to avoid punishment.

Through my many years of practice I have settled on one form of punishment that works for most patients. I ask the patient if he has an organization that he particularly hates. Typical answers include the Ku Klux Klan or the American Nazi Party. However, I have received answers from different patients that are diametrically opposite. One patient may hate a right to life organization while another patient may hate Planned Parenthood. One patient may hate the Democratic Party and another patient may hate the Republican Party. It generally does not matter to me what the organization is that the patient dislikes. I ask the patient for a certain amount of money. This varies depending on the patient's income. An average amount tends to be $100 or $200. This amount of cash is then placed in an envelope and addressed to the hated organization. I keep the envelope in the patient's chart. The agreement is rather simple. If the patient does not complete the assignment the envelope is mailed to the organization. This technique is very powerful and works about ninety percent of the time. Confession number fifty-five: There have been several occasions where I was not able to send off the envelope, even though I told the patient that I did. There is no way the American Nazi Party gets any money directly, or indirectly, from me.

When I first started using this technique I had a patient who was trying to complete a doctoral dissertation and was having difficulty writing. We established a contract where, if he did not write a certain number of pages on a daily basis, a check for $100 would be sent to the Ronald Reagan campaign fund. Needless to say the patient was anti-Reagan and anti-Republicans. After not completing his assignment one day the check was mailed. A few weeks later the patient came into my office with a huge bag full of mail and dumped it on my desk. "What is this?" I asked. The patient had been barraged with campaign literature from Reagan and the Republican Party. He even showed me an autographed picture of Nancy and Ronald Reagan that was inscribed, "Thank you for your generous contribution." The patient then went on to tell me that he had been inundated with calls from the Republican Party asking him for more money. The people calling him could not understand why he didn't want to contribute anymore. As it turned out this punishment was even more powerful than expected. He never missed completing another writing assignment.

January 14

When I arrived in my office today my mail was waiting for me. One piece of mail is particularly distressing. It is a bounced check from a patient. This tends to happen about four or five times a year. Most of the time I simply make a phone call. The patient is very apologetic and tells me he will put another check in the mail. There have been several times that the second check has bounced. One of the negative parts of my job is trying to collect money from patients that are no longer in treatment. I do have a billing service that will send them a bill each month. I am relatively sure that bills from psychologists are the last to be paid. I can see the patient trying to decide whether to pay his MasterCard with 437 percent interest due if not paid or the psychologist bill without interest. After a few months I sometimes ask the billing service to put reminders on the bill such as "past due." I think that most patients simply ignore the bills without ever reading them. I have had a desire in the past to write a short note on the bill stating that if the bill is not paid that the patient may get a visit from a hit man. After ignoring the bills and the reminders I generally try to call the patient to ask about the bill. Confession number fifty-six: I hope that the answering machine picks up so that I don't have to talk to the patient directly. I can then just leave a message that if the bill is not paid it will be sent to collections. I can't say I actually dislike sending the bills to collections. I don't believe that I will ever get paid from these patients, but I enjoy a slight revenge of screwing up their credit reports.

I used to go to small claims court to try to collect on unpaid bills. Patients would never show up, I would win the case and then I still would be unable to collect the judgment. I eventually figured out this was a waste of time and it was easier just to send the bills to a collection agency.

When I first began private practice I asked an experienced older colleague about the practice of billing patients. He told me that it was okay to bill old Jewish ladies because they would feel too guilty if they did not pay, but always to collect money from any attorney patients on the day of the session.

January 16

I have a new patient scheduled for today. Actually, it is a couple. They want to know how best to deal with the husband's seventy-year old mother who has hoarding OCD but does not think it is a problem. They describe a person who is a classical hoarder. She saves newspapers, magazines and food. She wraps up the food in paper and then saves it in her room. It is always very difficult to try to get patients to seek help when they don't believe they have a problem. An old psychologist joke goes: "How many psychologists does it take to change a light bulb?" The answer is: it all depends on whether the light bulb wants to be changed. It actually would be a major concern if everyone with psychological problems admitted it and entered treatment. There would not be enough therapists, even in L.A., to fill the need.

A few years ago a patient asked me how many people had OCD. I very intelligently quoted her the epidemiological statistics. She then asked me how many people were depressed. I again gave her my best estimate. She then asked about substance abuse, eating disorders, bipolar disorder, and schizophrenia. After trying to provide her the information as best as I could remember, she thought for a minute and asked, "Well then, how many people don't have anything wrong with them?" Confession number fifty-seven: I realized at that moment that having a psychological problem was probably the norm. I also realized that I would never run out of patients.

It is somewhat easier to get a child into therapy who does not want to come than a seventy-year old. However, I tried to picture the following conversation between my patients and the seventy-year old: "Mom, we think you have OCD. We think you are hoarding food and newspapers." "Son, just because I have last year's leftovers from Thanksgiving in my room is no reason to believe I have a problem." "Mom, those leftovers were from Easter, not Thanksgiving." "Son, I might get hungry sometimes when there is nothing else to eat in the house." "Mom, did you plan on sharing the food with the rats that are now residing in your room?"

The son in this case decided that it was no use in arguing with his mother and simply entered her room when she wasn't there and threw out most of the hoarded objects. This technique works very well for someone with OCD and some memory problems, since the mother could not possibly remember everything she had hoarded.

January 17

One of my patients today is a fifty-nine-year old married woman who I have been seeing for more than ten years. She originally came to therapy for a severe case of OCD. I believe I helped her somewhat with her problem but she basically refuses to do more work on the OCD. She informed me today that she is "going to be sixty years old. I'm not changing." So, you may ask why I continue to see this patient and why this patient continues to come to therapy on a weekly basis. The answer is simple - supportive therapy. Confession number fifty-eight: supportive therapy means I talk to this patient as if she was my good friend, and she pays me for it. In order to do this the first thing I must realize is that the patient is correct; she will not change. The next concept I must accept is that paying to talk to me is beneficial to this patient. The more obnoxious the patient, the less likely it is that they will have any friends to talk to for free.

I still try to follow a few simple rules when I do supportive therapy. I have to be a good listener and not interrupt the patient while she is speaking. Since this is not exactly natural for me, I have worked hard to develop and use this skill when needed. I also have to be non-judgmental. Some patients may make what I feel are absurd conclusions about their life that they do not want to change. For example, this patient has one of the worst marital relationships I have ever seen, but refuses to leave her husband. I also must be empathic. The patient needs to see that I am truly concerned about her situation even if I am truly not concerned. Patients in supportive therapy also tend to want to know more about the private life of the therapist. It is difficult to have a ten-year relationship with anyone and not answer his question about where you went on your recent vacation and how you enjoyed it.

I try to be objective whenever I do therapy. Being totally objective in this type of therapy relationship is nearly impossible. Every therapist brings his or her own values and experiences into the treatment setting. I guess it is good that I actually like my values; so that when I accidentally let them influence something I say to a patient, it is not likely to be harmful.

Several years ago one patient asked me when I was retiring. She appeared quite upset after I answered her question directly. It turns out she planned on being in supportive therapy for the rest of her life and didn't want to switch therapists.

The truth is that supportive therapy is much easier to do than cognitive-behavioral therapy. I don't have to prepare for the session, I don't have to figure out any assignments for the patient, and I don't have to worry about termination issues. In fact, when I actually like the patient who is receiving supportive therapy it feels like I am getting paid to talk to a friend.

January 20

Today is a national holiday, Martin Luther King Day. It is much easier to work on holidays that didn't exist when I was growing up. Most of my patients elect to come in today even though it is a holiday.

Early in the day I get a call from a potential new patient. In talking to her for five minutes it appears that she has a pretty serious anxiety disorder. After telling her about cognitive behavioral therapy I ask her if there are any other questions she has, or if she would like to make an appointment. She says there is just one more question; how old am I? I can answer the question two ways. I can tell the patient how old I am or try to avoid the answer by just telling her how many years I have been in practice. I never consider telling her that the answer is actually irrelevant to her getting good treatment. I decide to answer her question because I believe I am at the age where most patients think I am very experienced but not yet senile. I am sure that if I practiced into my sixties and seventies that some patients would not want to see me because they thought I was too old.

When I was just starting to see patients in my early twenties I was often perceived as being too young to be a therapist. I would get comments from middle-aged patients about how I was younger than their children. At that age I chose not to work with children because their parents would have asked me if I had children of my own. The question that patients who had children and needed parenting help invariably asked was, "How can you possible help me if you never had children of your own?" Confession number fifty-nine: At first I thought these patients were wrong. After all, I had read many child development books and had been supervised by a therapist with many years of experience in child therapy. After having my own child, I tend to think these people were correct. It is much easier to integrate the book learning with the actual life experience of raising a child.

A few years ago there was a television show called Doogie Hauser, M.D. Doogie was a child genius who graduated medical school at around age fourteen. I often wondered what a patient would do if she came into a clinic and were assigned a therapist that turned out to be a fourteen-year-old. I imagine the first response would be, "That is not what I meant when I said I needed to see a child psychologist." I used to like being told that I was awfully young to be a therapist. As I get older I don't think I will like being rejected because I was considered to be too old to be able to relate to the issues of a younger patient. Is age a relevant factor in choosing a therapist? In the type of therapy I do, I don't believe it is a very important factor, but if it makes the patient more comfortable to see someone his or her own age, then it can't hurt.

January 21

I had a new patient scheduled for 3 p.m. today and at 3:10 I decided to go into the waiting room to see if she was there. I do not have a receptionist, so when patients enter my waiting room there is a sign that says to push the button next to my name. When the patient pushes the button, a light goes on in my office indicating to me that the patient is waiting. Usually I tell patients about this light when I talk to them on the phone prior to their first appointment. However, some patients forget and some just think I will magically know when they arrive. Other patients think that a bell rings in my office and they are afraid to press it because it may disturb the patient in my office. Still other patients believe that this is some kind of intelligence test devised by the psychologist.

Having the light allows me to see when the patient arrives for his session. Most patients arrive either on time or a few minutes early. However, there is the occasional patient who arrives thirty or more minutes early. When the light goes on after I am already seeing a patient, I tend to ignore it unless it is during the first few minutes of a session. If it is early in the session I start to pray that I have not made a mistake and double-booked the time. Over the past ten years I can recall double booking about three or four sessions. Confession number sixty: When I realize the double booking is my mistake, I have the urge to ask both patients if they are interested in group therapy. Most of the time I just admit my mistake and offer the patient who hasn't yet started a free session. Usually this strategy works. The patient often feels like he has just won the lottery, and he walks out of my office smiling.

There are six therapists who share the office suite where I practice. This means there are often other patients in the waiting room. A few of the therapists see children. Occasionally, one of these potential adult neurotics does not like to share the waiting room with anyone else and decides to lock the entrance door from the inside of the waiting room. Most of the time, when one of my patients finds the door locked, he will wait in the hallway thinking that I have not yet arrived. Meanwhile, I am waiting in my office thinking the patient is late. I have this fantasy of someday catching one of these kids in the act of locking the waiting room door. I open the door and scare the hell out of the little neurotic. My colleague is grateful because the kid ends up needing more therapy.

Another problem in sharing the waiting room with other therapists is the issue of patients who are slobs. Some patients leave food lying around in the waiting room. Other patients spill their drinks on the carpet. It is interesting how none of the therapists believe it was their patient who spilled the drink. The patients never admit to it either. I walk into the waiting room and there is this giant wet coffee stain on the carpet. There are four patients sitting in the waiting room, each reading a magazine. I look at the coffee stain and ask does anyone know how this happened? No one answers. I sometimes think the threat of torture may get them to talk. "Ladies and Gentlemen, we will be staying here all night until someone admits to spilling the coffee."

January 22

I have not scheduled any patients today. I am out playing golf with some friends. I get the image in my head of the work police pulling me over. "Sir, please step out of the golf cart. Can I see your license and organizer, please?" I show the work police my psychology license, which I carry with me at all times just for emergencies like this. I also show them my electronic organizer with my daily schedule. They see that there are no patients scheduled for today. "Do you have a permit for not working today? I'm sorry sir, we are going to have to take you into your office until you can prove you shouldn't be working today."

January 23

I see another new patient today, NK. NK is having serious concerns about the direction of her life and what occupation she should pursue. She describes her work history to me that includes her most recent job as a bartender. She then tells me that many people have suggested that she go into psychology. I guess the assumption is that if you can listen to drunks at a bar that you have the prerequisite of being a good psychologist. Unfortunately, NK is not alone in her thinking. There are thousands of people in L.A. currently studying psychology and planning on going into practice. It seems that after every economic downturn the number of people going back to school in psychology increases. The technology failures in the past few years have probably contributed to the rise in psychology students. I used to work in a building that housed a psychology graduate program. In riding up the elevator one day with a colleague he remarked how everyone who was getting off on the floor that housed the graduate school looked like ex-real estate agents. Many of these students are bored housewives who figure they could start a little counseling practice on the side. Many of them never finish their degree or ever pass their licensing exam. Very few ever become successful therapists. The majority of people who go back to school at a later age become Marriage and Family Therapists.

There is a pecking order among mental health practitioners: psychiatrists, psychologists, social workers, marriage and family therapists and then bartenders. Confession number sixty-one: Psychologists like to think they are better than all of the other disciplines. I start to foam at the mouth when a patient asks me if his psychiatrist could do the behavior therapy so that he won't have to see two different practioners. For right now I don't discourage NK from the idea of becoming a psychologist. In fact, it appears she is even more interested in the idea at the end of the session when she finds out what my rate is.

January 24

One of the things I have done over the past few days is to call patients whose accounts are overdue. One of the patients I call answers the phone and, as soon as she hears that it is me, she tells me that she gets the feeling she is going to be a little bit poorer. Several patients claim that they have never received a bill even though my billing office claims that they have sent them numerous bills. The last patient I call is WO. WO was a patient about three or four months ago who completed therapy but did not pay for the last two sessions. Just last week she paged me to tell me she was starting to have panic attacks. I spent a great deal of time with her on the phone over the weekend and told her to call me when she was done having her physical tests and the doctors had assured her that she was just having anxiety. During the week the bill that was sent to this patient was returned to me with an incorrect address. So today I need to call the patient to find out her correct address. I initially ask her how she is doing. After letting me know the results of her medical test she informs me that she has started therapy with a new therapist. I have difficulty understanding this action and I am angry. She pages me in an emergency and then goes into therapy with someone else. Confession number sixty-two: I have a strong desire to just tell her "where to go." Instead, I wish her luck and get off the phone as quickly as possible. I also realize that I probably will not get paid if I told her how I felt about her actions. I feel used. Psychoanalysts call this counter transference. Humanistic psychologists would probably tell me that I am in touch with my feelings. Cognitive therapists would want to know what thought I had that led to this emotion. And, finally, Tony Soprano would want to know if I wanted to hire a hit man. I guess I would not feel as bad if I charged patients for phone time as attorneys do. I could have a little stopwatch next to the phone to time all of these additional therapeutic contacts. I could then collect on a per minute rate. I think it would drastically reduce patient phone calls.

Another patient leaves me two four-minute messages today. On his third message he admits to having been told that his messages are too long, so he wrote this new one out prior to calling me. Only problem was that it took him forty-five minutes to write the new message. I want to inform any psychotherapy patient, or potential patient, of the correct answering machine message to leave your therapist. "Dr. Help, this is Jane Patient. My phone number is (310) 555-4356. You can reach me at that number between three and seven p.m. Thank you." Using this message, and of course your own name and phone numbers, will ensure the everlasting gratitude of your therapist.

January 27

I received a call today from Fox Television asking me to send them some tapes of me being interviewed and of me doing therapy. They initially did not say what the tapes would be used for. I asked the first person who called and she told me I would have to speak to her boss. When her boss got on the phone she repeated that she wanted tapes of me. I said I needed to be very blunt and I asked, "What's in it for me?" At that point she told me that she was putting together a new TV reality show similar to Dr. Phil. Confession number sixty-three: I start to have grandiose thoughts about my own TV show. Dr. Jerry may not sound bad after all. I will now have to look at all the tapes of previous television interviews and pick out the most impressive pieces.

I received another call today from a prospective new patient. What makes this patient different is that he is a psychologist. It is definitely an ego boost to have another therapist as one of your patients. I have treated about a dozen psychologists and psychiatrists through the years. I treated one psychologist many years ago who never paid my bill and his account had to be sent to collections. After this new patient made an appointment with me he asked how much I charged. After telling him, he responded, "That's more than I charge." I am not sure how I would have felt if he said, "Oh, that's very reasonable."

January 28

After practicing psychology for such a long time I am truly shocked to discover a problem that I have never encountered before. Today I had such an experience.

A new patient complained of being anxious in a very specific situation - anytime she hears anything to do with the Democratic Party. Mention former President Clinton and she starts to sweat and become very nervous. I decide that I can treat her for this problem, but I wonder to myself if there are other similar problems out there. If there is someone fearful of Democrats there must also be people fearful of Republicans. Maybe there are people fearful of New Yorkers, fearful of psychologists, fearful of people named James, fearful of Italian food. I guess any fear is possible. The National Geographic Channel recently ran a series of shows on phobias. They showed people fearful of flying, fearful of heights, fearful of snakes, and with many other common fears. They also did an episode on fear of clowns. They showed an adult who seemed to have a complete panic attack when a clown entered the room. Confession number sixty-four: I have never treated anyone who has a fear of clowns and don't know any other psychologist who ever has treated this problem. What if a patient who has a fear of

Republicans also has a fear of clowns? Would I have to eventually get a picture of George Bush in a clown suit, or is that redundant?

I am trying to decide what the worst thing would be for a person who is afraid of Republicans. In my mind having to listen to Rush Limbaugh might be the ultimate fear. Some people may actually consider that cruel and unusual punishment rather than treatment.

Another patient today tells me, economically, she feels like Campbell's soup. What the hell does that mean? I think I am pretty bright, but I just don't get it. I have the urge to ask her if she feels more like Chicken Noodle or Chunky Vegetable.

January 30

I thought it might be interesting to update you on the six patients I saw today. My first patient LO continues to struggle with his OCD fears of something being physically wrong with him. I try to convince him not to call the doctor to get any more reassurances about the results of his latest visit. He wants to know how I know that there is nothing physically wrong with him and that his fears are just his OCD. I tell him that if his arm were dangling by a tendon and blood was spurting out all over the place that he wouldn't be asking me for advice. If he asks me, it must be OCD.

My second patient MW continues not to be motivated to make any changes. He comes to therapy today with his mother. Every time I open the waiting room door and see his mother I know that MW hasn't done any therapeutic homework the past two weeks. I put on my best cheerleading outfit to try to convince him to make some changes. As usual he leaves the session all charged up to try some new things. Just call me Tony Robbins Tarlow.

The next patient, YD, another OCD patient, can't stop talking the entire session. I have difficulty completing my therapeutic agenda, but I am able to give my voice a nice rest.

I then get to see HN, a twenty-six-year-old male patient who has been to two previous therapy sessions for panic disorder. My goal today is to teach him relaxation training. The only problem is I have done this about 2,000 times in the past thirty years and doing it again makes me feel like I am working at McDonalds flipping my 2,000th hamburger. I try to find new ways of presenting the relaxation exercise, but it basically turns out the same. Do you think any patients would care if I automated the procedure and just had them watch a videotape of me explaining the technique? I could even serve popcorn while they were watching.

Next comes TH. TH was one of my patients who had a contract to complete her elevator practice during the week. She informs me that she failed and I now have to send her money to her ex-boyfriend who she hates. If that didn't motivate her to do the work, I don't know what will. I try some paradoxical therapy with her. I tell her I don't think she really wants to get better. This technique fails when she agrees with me.

My sixth patient is LB, who immediately starts sobbing upon entering my office. I know I am in for a long session. I hope my Kleenex supply lasts. There is nothing worse than running out of Kleenex when you have a sobbing patient in the room. Confession number sixty-five: I hate it when patients go over to take some Kleenex and half the box comes out at once. It actually makes some patients cry even more. I have thought of putting one of those pop up snakes in the Kleenex box just as a practical joke. It might distract the patient from the thoughts that led to crying. The smart female patients who plan on crying never wear eye makeup to the session. The patients who wear excessive makeup tend to leave the session looking like a circus clown gone bad.

January 31

A couple has made an appointment today to talk about their twenty-six-year-old son who has OCD. In the middle of the session they tell me about the therapy he is receiving. If what they tell me is true, their son has not received the appropriate treatment. I always ask who the therapist is and feel particularly conflicted if it is someone I know. In this case I have never heard of the therapist. Confession number sixty-six: I actually take some pleasure in telling patients that their therapist may have been incompetent. It is even more pleasurable when the therapist claims to be a cognitive behavior therapist and appears to not be doing the therapy correctly. I can't picture passing myself off as an expert in a particular therapy and really not knowing what I am doing. Maybe I could try it for a day; perhaps on April Fool's day. At least after the session I could just tell the patient I was only kidding.

I try to educate this couple on what they should look for in a therapist for their son. They are very appreciative and thank me immensely at the end of the session.

I am preparing to go to New York City for the weekend and I use this upcoming trip in helping some of my depressed patients gain some perspective. It is about eighty degrees in L.A. today and about thirty-five degrees and raining in New York. I try to convince my patients that I should be the one who is depressed, not them.

CHAPTER 5
February

February 3

Today a patient asked me one of the three stupidest questions any patient has ever asked. I have to admit this question has been asked several times before. I do not know which of the four questions that follow is the most stupid. Therefore, I would like you, the reader, to vote for your favorite.

1. Do you accept cash?

2. (Upon referring a patient to one of my assistants:) Is she as good a therapist as you are?

3. (A new patient's question at the first session:) Can you cure my fear of flying by the end of the week when I have a flight scheduled?

4. (A patient's question with ten minutes left in the session:) Can I ask you another question?

This is how I answered each of these questions.

1. Yes, I do.

2. She has a great deal of experience in treating patients with similar problems.

3. I may be able to help you feel a little
more relaxed for the flight.

4. Of course you can ask another question.

Confession number sixty-seven: After some careful thought this is what I should have said.

1. Yes, but only if it is in unmarked $20 bills.

2. No, she is a lot better. In fact
she supervises my cases.

3. Of course I can cure you by Friday. But first I
have to find a cure for AIDS by Wednesday.

4. I know this is your time and you are paying
for it, but I do not allow questions in
the last ten minutes of any session.

February 4

I have another new patient today who wants an evaluation. In completing these first time evaluations I always ask about the other therapists the patient has seen. This patient has seen a number of psychologists and psychiatrists that I know and who have excellent reputations. He tells me about one psychiatrist who he saw for many years who he felt was very good, but he had to quit seeing him because the therapist would always talk about his own OCD and how he was treating it. I never knew this psychiatrist had OCD and I am not sure he would want me to know. However, although a therapist can't reveal information about their patient without the patient's consent, the reverse is not true. Tell a patient something about yourself and it may get published in the National Enquirer the next week. I can't sue the patient for breaking confidentiality. This interaction again leads to a series of bad dreams where I envision headlines in the National Enquirer: Prominent L.A. Psychologist admits to giving rude driver the finger. Maybe I should be less revealing in sessions.

This patient also tells me that he has seen only one psychologist for five sessions of therapy and that the person was the worst therapist imaginable. Confession number sixty-eight: I need to ask who the therapist is. He asks me if I want to know her name and I respond that I do. It turns out to be a psychologist I know fairly well. I file the information away in my head and try to ignore it unless I hear more unfavorable reports about his therapist. I often wonder what some of the patients who stopped seeing me said about me to their next therapist?

Another confidentiality issue arose today. I received a call from a woman who wanted to get her son into therapy. She asked me if it would be okay if they didn't bill their insurance company. I assured her that I do accept cash and asked why she was so concerned about the insurance company not knowing about the treatment. She told me that she was a practicing psychiatrist and she did not trust the insurance company to keep the information confidential. Just another strong endorsement of the insurance industry. My goal is to hear one nice thing about the insurance industry before I retire. I take that back. I would like to retire before the next century.

I received an e-mail today from another psychologist regarding billing the patient's insurance. This psychologist received a check for $3,025 from the insurance company for one of his patients. He returned the check to the insurance company with the following reply: "I like to think of myself as a versatile and energetic professional, but I could not have delivered Ms. X's baby last June 11. I had just returned from a psychology conference in New Orleans and was simply too busy to attend to her needs."

February 6

In reading a magazine for therapists a few weeks ago I discovered a new product - the invisible clock. It looked intriguing so I ordered one and it arrived yesterday. Today will be the first day I attempt to use it. This product was specifically designed to be able to tell a therapist how much time is left in the session without making it obvious to the patient that you are looking at the clock. It looks like a regular pager that can be worn on your belt. It gives off slight vibrations at preset times. You can set it to vibrate at the halfway point in the session, five minutes before the end of the session, and when the session ends. I decided to order one so that I can reduce the number of clocks I have in my office. I anticipate several problems. I must train myself not to jump out of my chair when the pager vibrates. It would be very difficult explaining such behavior to the patient. If you don't look at the clock and you tell the patient their session is over and the patient asks how you knew the time, do you tell her about the invisible clock? I imagine telling the patient that after doing therapy for more than thirty years that my brain automatically knows when forty-five minutes have elapsed.

After spending the requisite hour figuring out how to program the invisible clock, I use it for the entire day. It works great, but I still end up looking at all the clocks in my office. I think I am very conditioned to look at the clocks and it may take me a while to break the habit. Confession number sixty-nine: I have the desire to give the invisible clock to the patients when they walk into the session. I could have them wear it and they could then be better able to figure out how much time they have left in the session. However, I would like to add a small electric current to be used when the patient exceeds his time. The longer he goes past forty-five minutes, the stronger the electric shock.

One of my patients today was TH who was continuing to work on her elevator phobia. In trying to avoid taking an elevator during the week, TH walked down the stairs only to find the exit door locked. Ironically, she was now trapped in the staircase. She had to bang on doors for about ten minutes before anyone let her out. Maybe this will now motivate her to take elevators. I am sure that someday an elevator phobic will trip on the stairs and seriously injure himself.

February 7

One of my patients today is VZ. VZ is a thirty-five-year-old single male with a probable diagnosis of borderline personality disorder. This is not a problem I frequently treat, but occasionally a patient with an anxiety disorder also has borderline personality disorder. I could review all of the diagnostic criteria for this disorder for you, but I will boil down my diagnostic criteria to one: You intensely dislike the patient, never want to see or talk to him again, and try to figure out a way of getting the patient out of your practice. Generally, getting rid of a patient like this is referred to as "dumping" the patient. However, I have learned through the years that there are a number of therapists who actually enjoy working with borderline patients. I think they view these patients as a challenge. Confession number seventy: I view jumping off the roof of my office building and landing safely on my feet as a challenge, but I would never do it. I view having my tooth pulled without sedation as a challenge, but I would never do it.

I used to pray that borderline patients would not show up for their sessions. However, after this happened a few times and the patients accused me of giving them the wrong appointment time, I stopped praying. I used to hope that the patient just showed up late and I would have a shorter session. However, a borderline's sense of entitlement would lead to her being unable to leave your office until she had her full forty-five minutes. I try to gently convince such patients that I am not an expert on treating this condition and they may be better off transferring to another therapist. This strategy often fails because the patient then demands all of her money back for previous sessions.

My most memorable borderline patient was a woman I saw several years ago. She was referred by another psychologist who I used to assume liked me. Initially she told me that she needed some stress management treatment. Everything was going fine for a few sessions. On her fourth session she entered my office, looked at a file on my desk and asked: "Is that my file?" I told her it was and then she immediately demanded to take the file and leave the session. This was a request I had never heard from any previous patient. I told her I would gladly copy the information for her but that I was legally required to retain the original. She became so infuriated and agitated that I actually had to call the security guard to have her removed from my office. I called her to refer her to another therapist. The referral went to one of those individuals who think treating borderline patients is a challenge. It was also a therapist I did not personally like. That is when the real "fun" started. She proceeded to page me about forty to fifty times per day. She would fill up my answering machine with Spanish music recordings during the night. I must admit this was an ingenious mode of revenge. When I would call my answering machine in the morning I would have over thirty messages. I would have to listen to the beginning of each one in case a real patient message was interspersed with the Spanish music. I decided to not return any of her calls, hoping that she would just go away. Unfortunately, that did not happen. She started to stalk me. She waited outside my office and tried to get into the exit door. She followed me to the tennis courts and actually threatened to kill me if I didn't give her the original records and return all of the money that she had spent on therapy. At that point I decided to get a restraining order, which a judge agreed was warranted. I never heard from the patient again, but I did get a call from the therapist I referred the patient to. He wanted to know how to get a restraining order against this patient. Apparently the patient started stalking him. I later found out that this patient had seven restraining orders against her from previous therapists. This is the ultimate borderline personality disorder!

February 10

I have a new patient today who told me about her previous therapists. One of her previous therapists revealed a great deal of personal information to the patient. For a long time therapists have debated the value and use of revealing information about their own personal lives to patients. Some therapists believe this is inappropriate. Other therapists believe some personal information can be helpful to the therapeutic process. I have no problem in telling a patient that my father died several years ago if I am trying to help a patient deal with the loss of a parent. I have no problem revealing frustrations I may be having in dealing with my teenage son if I am trying to help a patient deal more effectively with his or her teenager. I would like to believe that any personal information that I reveal to a patient is relevant to the patient's problem. The only exception to this might be if the patient asks about my vacation or what I did over the weekend. I do feel comfortable in telling the patient the positives in answering these types of personal questions. However, I do not believe it is helpful to tell a patient about negative events or crises in my life. If a patient starts a session with asking me how I am, I generally don't let the patient know that my mother is in the hospital, my daughter just got arrested, and the IRS is auditing my last tax return. I also would not let the patient know that I was so depressed I didn't want to come to work today. This is the type of personal information that my new patient received from her previous therapist. If you are a patient and a therapist tells you this information, what do you do? How do you then immediately start talking about your own problems? Confession number seventy-one: If a therapist told me all of that inappropriate personal information I would immediately ask to switch chairs with him and then inform him of my therapy rate.

February 11

One of my patients today is CB. CB has a fairly common problem; she pulls her hair out. The diagnosis for this problem is "trichotillomania." This is the best name of any psychiatric disorder. Isn't it bad enough to have to tell people that you pull your hair out without convincing them that trichotillomania is not a sexually transmitted disease? It is very easy to spot a person with trichotillomania. They are the ones who never take their hats off and never go swimming. Most patients with this problem tend to pull out the hair on their head. Some patients pull out their eyelashes or eyebrows. A few patients pull out their pubic hair.

One of the treatments for trichotillomania is called habit reversal. One component of habit reversal is teaching patients to use a competing response every time they have the urge to pull a hair. Typical competing responses include squeezing a stress ball, rubbing on a worry stone, or even pulling on a koosh ball. I have had patients ask me if this was just substituting one bad habit for another. I tell my patients that in all the years I have practiced I have never had a patient come into therapy and tell me she was addicted to squeezing a stress ball and it was ruining his life.

For many patients with trichotillomania the problem occurs as a result of high levels of stress. I often find it interesting what self-destructive things people do to relieve their stress. I have had patients who pick their skin until it bleeds, patients who grind their teeth until they get headaches, and patients who eat until they vomit. Why can't these people learn to control stress like the rest of us? Just get a drink.

Although trichotillomania is the best name of a psychiatric disorder it is not the most unusual disorder. My choice for the most bizarre disorder is pica. Pica is a childhood disorder that essentially consists of the ingestion of non-nutritive items. The most common items ingested by people with this problem include feces and paper. Confession number seventy-two: If I were to take a pica patient with me to a hoarder's house I've often wondered if he might be able to just eat the papers that the hoarder was trying to discard.

February 13

One of my patients today has a fear of harming other people or herself. She is so afraid of these aggressive thoughts that she has removed all the knives, scissors, and razor blades from her house. She actually broke up with her last boyfriend because she was afraid she would harm him. These are actually OCD symptoms and are not just the ramblings of a psychotic individual. People with these sorts of obsessions are afraid these things will happen but they never follow through on the thoughts. I have had patients who were afraid they would kill their spouse, their children, or even themselves. Remember the treatment I described for OCD - exposure and response prevention. A typical exposure session for a patient with a fear of stabbing their spouse would be to hold a sharp knife close to his spouse. I tell the patient to make sure and inform his spouse of the assignment. Patients continually want to know how I know they will not stab his spouse. I tell them that if they actually hate their spouse or they have previously served twenty years for stabbing their first spouse that I wouldn't ask them to do this exposure. Confession number seventy-three: I have this nightmare that a brilliant psychopath wants to kill his wife and discovers this treatment for OCD. He comes to my office and I give him the assignment to hold a butcher knife to his wife's back. He ends up killing his wife and blaming me. "My psychologist told me to do it. He told me it was just an obsession and that I would never kill her. Why did I listen to him?" This almost sounds like a good plot for a movie.

February 14

It is Valentine's Day today and love is in the air. I have actually had only a few patients in all my years of practice state that they were in love with me. In my business, this reaction is known as "transference."

I would like to believe that it is because I do short-term treatment that this reaction occurs so infrequently in my practice. If I fell in love with one of my patients it would be referred to as "countertransference" or a felony in the state of California.

A few years ago a very overweight patient left me a message admitting she was in love with me. She wondered if at the next session I could hypnotize her into believing that I was very ugly.

Occasionally a patient views me as perfect and without any flaws. Confession number seventy-four: They obviously did not have a chance to talk to my father when he was alive. They clearly have not talked to my teenage son.

I received candy from two patients today. Both of them appear to be happily married and not interested in me, so I gladly accepted the candy.

February 17

My 1 p.m. patient today is SF. SF has a very specific type of social phobia. He is afraid to urinate in public. This happens to be a very common problem specific to men. If you are with a male friend and you both go the restroom and your friend chooses to use a stall rather than a urinal, it is a good bet that he has this social phobia. Patients with this phobia often dread going to concerts or sporting venues where the urinals are just metal troughs. Now, you may think that this fear has to do with men being uncomfortable with the size or shape of their penis. Actually men who have this problem are afraid they will not be able to urinate in front of others and these other people will see this and make fun of them. People with this fear view urinating in public as a performance. Being unable to urinate is similar to being unable to talk when attempting to give a speech.

Some men hide this problem and never get help. They use stalls in public restrooms and often avoid going out in public. SF has decided to get help in overcoming this problem. He is about halfway through treatment and our current session involves his using the public restroom in my building while I am waiting outside the door. He believes I could hear him if he was able to urinate and that I would know if he was unable to urinate. I would really like to get SF to the point where he would believe that the only people who actually care whether or not he is able to urinate in public are other men with the same problem. Nobody is looking at him. Nobody is listening to him. Confession number seventy-five: Not only am I not listening outside the door, I actually use the time to complete some unfinished notes from a previous patient. I would become a bit concerned if he didn't come out of the bathroom after a few minutes.

February 18

One of the patients today in the UCLA program has a diagnosis of body dysmorphobic disorder or BDD for short. BDD is a preoccupation with a certain body part or aspect of appearance. If you continually think about whether your nose is too big, your breasts are too small or your hair is too thin you may have BDD. I have also treated people who have felt their head is too big, their spine is too curved, their gums are protruding too far or their skin is the wrong color. Treating BDD in L.A. is not easy. It tends to be difficult to convince some patients that their perception of their appearance is distorted. It is likely that ninety percent of the population of the Westside of L.A. has a little BDD. BDD is similar to OCD in that patients engage in compulsive behaviors. Probably the two most common compulsions are looking in the mirror and making multiple doctor appointments. Some patients have many plastic surgeries in an attempt to "fix" the problem.

One of the treatments for BDD is very similar to OCD. I first take pictures of the patient. Then I use the computer to distort the aspect of the patient's appearance he is concerned about. For example, if a patient is concerned about losing his hair I will make him bald in the picture. If a patient is concerned that his head is too big I will blow up his head in the picture. Confession number seventy-six: I get a great deal of pleasure in "playing" with these pictures. The more realistic the pictures look the more likely the treatment is to be successful. Patients are then instructed to look at the pictures until the distorted image no longer produces anxiety.

I have talked to plastic surgeons who have been contacted by my patients to perform surgery on the particular body part the patient is concerned about. I have yet to find a plastic surgeon willing to turn down a patient because of BDD. The general attitude of the plastic surgeon is if the patient wants to change his or her appearance, and the patient is willing to pay, then the surgery must be okay. I had one patient who actually had nine nose jobs. It seems his nose was never exactly right after each surgery.

February 20

Helping people get better is what keeps me going. If patients did not improve I don't think I could have lasted so long in this profession. Most of the time you know when a patient has improved. If a patient has a fear of flying and had not flown in thirty-five years but he is able to take a flight now, he has improved. If a patient was having six panic attacks a day and now is having none, he has improved. What I often do not get from patients is how the improvement has changed their lives. Today I contacted an ex-patient to ask if she would be willing to talk to a current patient about her success in treatment. The ex-patient said she would be glad to do that because the treatment had changed her life and I was responsible for that. Confession number seventy-seven: After telling the patient that she was responsible for the change because she did all of the work, I smiled to myself knowing that I was the one who actually got her to do the correct "work." When patients tell you how much your help has changed their life, it is very reinforcing. If you are a patient and want your therapist to really like you, tell him how much the treatment is helping. Most of the time he will believe you even if he thought the treatment wasn't helping very much. He then will likely be more attentive during your sessions.

There are always certain patient successes that tend to stand out more than others. I always feel very good about getting people to fly who have not flown in years. I feel great about getting people to drive on freeways if they have been avoiding that for years. However, some of the OCD patients I have treated whose lives were basically controlled by their symptoms and who are now fully functional stand out more than the other successes.

February 21

I saw another adolescent patient today. She told me that she was in big trouble. Her mother had asked her to not have anyone over at the house but the patient, ignoring her mother's rule, invited some friends over. The mother eventually found out about the incident and gave this patient one of the most severe punishments I have ever heard of. For an entire month my patient could not drive her brand new Mercedes and would have to drive the one-year-old SUV instead. After contemplating whether to report the parents for child abuse I decided to offer them some additional possible punishments that they could use the next time they needed to discipline their child. (1) No watching the 53" plasma TV, only the 40" Sony, (2) on the next trip to Hawaii, the patient would be forced to travel business class rather than first class, and (3) no takeout food from five-star restaurants for the next week. There are just some times that one must use "tough love" as a parent.

I also had an OCD patient today who appeared to take a little skip over the threshold as she entered my office. This may go unnoticed by most people, but I am very sure that the skipping over the threshold was a compulsion. After a few minutes of the session she asked if she could do something. I asked her if she wanted to do another compulsion and she responded that she did. Letting a patient do a compulsion in my presence is somewhat similar to allowing an alcoholic to drink a beer during the session. When patients ask me if they can do a compulsion in my office I like to ask them if they want to get better. I figure if they say no, I can tell them it is okay to do the compulsion. This patient stated she wanted to get better but was experiencing so much anxiety that if she didn't do the compulsion now she would be unable to eat today or sleep tonight. I had no desire to physically restrain her so I watched as she left my office and then re-entered. This patient's obsession was that she had to have a good thought when entering my office or else she had to go back and do it again. Having a good thought to replace a bad thought is a rather common OCD symptom. Confession number seventy-eight: I tried this compulsion for a few days, just to see how it felt. I had to stop doing it when I ran out of good thoughts.

February 24

I have a new patient today who is an actress. Her problem is social anxiety. She has no anxiety when performing but gets extremely anxious in any non-work social situation. The key symptom for most people with social anxiety is a fear of being judged or evaluated by others. Therefore, it is interesting that an actress, who is constantly judged by others, would have difficulty with this problem. It has been interesting for me to see some of the problems that patients complain of and I try to reconcile their problems with their occupations. I have treated famous actors who have stage fright. I have treated a pilot for fear of flying. I have treated a medical student for fear of blood. I have treated comedians and comedy writers for depression and I have treated physicians for fear of AIDS. Confession number seventy-nine: I have never treated an attorney for fear of lying.

I also had my first supervision session with a new psychological assistant today. About seventy-five percent of the hour was spent discussing business issues. One can get a great education in clinical psychology at most universities. However, they still do not teach you how to survive in private practice. Most universities are still under the assumption that most clinical psychology graduate students are only interested in a career in research and teaching. These schools often end up producing very bright and competent therapists who have no idea of how to bill a patient's insurance company. As much as any psychologist in private practice enjoys what he is doing, there is still a business to run. Running a successful business is generally not the reason most students chose a career in psychology. Many of these students actually turn out to be terrible business people. I had one friend in private practice who I considered a terrific clinician. He always saw more patients than I do, but continually complained about "making ends meet." He also routinely forgot to bill patients or insurance companies for work that he performed.

February 25

I had a very bad session with one of my patients today. I am pretty sure that the patient didn't know it was a bad session, but I knew. You may wonder what constitutes a bad session for a cognitive-behavioral therapist. It was not that I wasn't listening to the patient. It was not that I didn't understand what the patient was saying. It just seemed that every little intervention I tried with the patient failed. I wanted the patient to give me a short description of his fears. After twenty minutes of describing his fears I had to interrupt him. After a while I just sort of gave up and let the patient talk for the rest of the session. Thankfully, I don't think I have very many sessions like this one. Confession number eighty: I feel like telling this kind of patient that I did a lousy job and I wasn't charging him for the session. Luckily this thought passes quickly and I accept the check. I wonder what I would do if a patient said, "Dr. Tarlow, you did a very poor job this session. Are you really going to charge me?" I had one patient many years ago in the UCLA OCD program whose father was paying the bill. At the end of the six-week program I sent him a bill for $1,200 for treatment for his son. He sent me a very nasty letter back telling me that his son did not improve enough and therefore he was not paying my bill. I tried sending him to collections, but after he threatened to sue me I told the collection agency to stop trying to collect the bill. Even though I thought I would win in court it wasn't worth it to me to pursue it. If you ever want to get your money back from a psychologist just threaten to sue him for malpractice. He will gladly refund your payments rather than go to court or have to defend himself to a licensing board.

February 27

One of my patients today is a compulsive shoplifter. Shoplifting is a problem that has some similarities to OCD. The main difference is that the shoplifter derives pleasure from the behavior but for the person with OCD the compulsion serves to reduce anxiety. I have treated about ten shoplifters over the course of my career. After treating a few who were referred by the legal system I realized that the only shoplifters I wanted to see were the ones who were self- referred and did not have to complete treatment to satisfy their sentencing. Shoplifters have definitely given me an education on some of their criminal behaviors. I have worked with a shoplifter who acquired every piece of furniture, clothing, and even her food by stealing it. One shoplifter showed me how she was able to simply walk out of department stores with large objects. If you see a person walking down the street carrying a 36-inch TV it may be one of my patients. I had one shoplifter who continually stole things from stores and then returned them to get store credit. Confession number eighty-one: I have thought of removing objects from my waiting room prior to seeing some of these shoplifters. None of the shoplifters ever stole anything from my office, but I must admit I would always check the waiting room after they left.

One of the amazing things about shoplifters is their ability to justify the behavior. Very often they will tell you that they are not really harming anyone or even that they deserve to have what they just stole. Many of these patients come from wealthy backgrounds and could afford to buy everything that they stole. One of my patients did not even need any of the things she stole. She just gave away most of the objects as presents. I have yet to treat a male shoplifter. I know they are out there. I have seen them in Ralphs sampling the bulk candy without paying for it.

My success rate for curing shoplifters is not so good. I try to have these patients practice shopping in stores they have previously shoplifted in without stealing anything. I want to teach them that they can resist the urge to shoplift. Many of these patients don't want to change and they drop out of treatment. Many of them believe that they are much smarter than the store employees and either will never get caught or would just get off with a hand slap. I am sure Winona Ryder, who is not one of my patients, had similar thoughts.

February 28

I am sick and feel crappy today. I have a sore throat and this time I have laryngitis. I did not cancel any patients today but I was sure hoping a few of them forget about their appointments. I was thinking very seriously of telling all my patients that I will give them fifty percent off my rates today. After all, I probably could only listen today. Why don't psychologists have sales? Every other type of business has sales. Why don't you ever see an advertisement for psychological services stating: "Special one day sale? All sessions fifty percent off." What about a going out of business sale? "Psychologist retiring. All sessions discounted till retirement date. Save big!" Family discounts might also work. "Is your family paying too much for psychotherapy? Dr. Tarlow now offers family therapy packages. One parent and one child twenty-five percent off. One parent and two children thirty percent off. Two parents and one child twenty percent off. Please inquire about our three parent specials for non-intact families." Confession number eighty-one: I think therapists could also give out frequent shrink awards as a way of rewarding loyal patients, just like the airlines reward good passengers. How about forty-five shrink points for each forty-five-minute session? How about bonus shrink points for patients who do their assignments or pay at each session? How about double shrink points for patients who pay in cash? Points could be redeemed for free sessions, depending on space availability. You probably would have to have blackout hours when the patient was unable to redeem points. Points could also be used for a free IQ test or maybe some added phone consultations.

As the day wears on my voice becomes weaker and weaker. The last few patients probably should get seventy percent off.

CHAPTER 6
March

March 3

I get an e-mail today from a person having bad panic attacks. He asks about a dozen different questions in the e-mail. I assume that the test is that the therapist who answers his e-mail and actually responds to all twelve questions is the winner and will be the lucky one to get his business. One of the questions he asks is whether there are any holistic or herbal remedies for panic attacks. He also wants to know about changing his diet. Some patients believe that the proper diet can cure any problem, even an emotional one. Confession number eighty-two: I want to e-mail him back and tell him that the right amount of potato chips and ice cream have been shown to completely eliminate panic attacks. The chance that this diet would actually work is probably about thirty-three percent. That is the typical placebo response with many studies. I have always been impressed by the power of the human mind to make changes when a person truly believes in the treatment.

I have had other patients ask me what I thought about psychics. Even though the words psychic and psychologist contain the same first five letters it does not mean that we have anything else in common. My opinion of the accuracy of psychics is about the same as the Magic Eight Ball. However, the Magic Eight Ball is a lot cheaper.

Later in the day my wife asks me if I received a long e-mail from some guy with panic attacks. She had received the same e-mail! He fooled me. The e-mail started out, "Dr. Tarlow." I thought he took the time to write just to me. How narcissistic of me to believe that. I never would have responded to him if I knew he sent the e-mail to 150 different therapists.

March 4

While doing therapy there was an extended blackout in my office today. This is the first time this has happened to me in all the years I have been in practice. I discover another reason I should be grateful to be a psychologist. My office has large windows and there is plenty of natural light. The blackout does not affect my ability to perform my business one iota. Think about the low overhead involved in psychotherapy. A room, two chairs and a box of Kleenex. No office staff and no office machines are required. I know therapists whose cell phones double as their office phone. No billing service is needed if you collect each session.

I saw a patient today who informed me that she had developed a new obsession. She was now afraid of contracting HIV. This happens to be a very common obsession that I have treated many times before. Just like the Boy Scouts, psychologists should be prepared. Part of my preparation for this obsession is to keep a vile of blood in my desk drawer. This allows me to surprise the patient by whipping out the vile and asking her if she is able to hold it in her hands. Most patients just refuse. Some patients ask me where the blood came from, but most really don't care. Confession number eighty-three: It is my blood that one of the nurses in the OCD program agreed to draw and let me keep. It is the second vile of blood I have had in my office. The first one I lent to a patient and he never returned it. Given the price I paid to get my own blood drawn, it was the last time I loaned it to a patient. Having the blood right there in my drawer reassures patients that I am familiar with this obsession and that I must be very experienced.

When I was in graduate school I was taught to have similar "props" at hand to treat various phobias. For numerous reasons the phobia that was the most common in psychological journal articles was fear of snakes. I truly believed that all psychologists should have a rubber snake in their desk drawer to help evaluate the patient's fear of snakes. I had my rubber snake for ten years before I realized no one ever comes into therapy in L.A. with a fear of snakes. One of the reasons the problem was so highly investigated is that it is a very common fear. However, in L.A. the fear generally does not interfere with a person's life.

When I teach classes about the treatment of fears I often bring in a jar of spiders into the class to help evaluate the student's fear of them. I generally spend the evening before the lecture collecting spiders from my garage. I bring them into class and ask the entire class how anxious they are around spiders. I then take out the jar and assess their actual fear. Numerous students who said they had no fear still refused to stick their hand in the jar.

March 6

One of my patients today was just released from the psychiatric hospital only yesterday. She was hospitalized because she was threatening to kill herself. She didn't even page me but went directly to the emergency room because she was afraid that she might harm herself. One of the worst fears of many psychologists is to have one of their patients commit suicide. Although I have had many depressed patients throughout my practice I have yet to have a current patient commit suicide. I did have one ex-patient kill herself three months after she had dropped out of treatment. I've had to have a few patients hospitalized to prevent them from killing themselves. As a therapist, it is hard to keep from feeling a bit like a failure when a patient kills himself. Most patients would never blame the therapist for their suicide. I heard a number of stories of patients actually jumping out of their therapist's window in my previous office building, which was twenty-one stories high and had sliding windows in each office that could be opened. I for one view that as the ultimate insult to a therapist. "Not only could you not help me, but I will make sure that you never forget me."

Another patient I'm seeing today has also had recurring suicidal thoughts. I can never predict whether she will come into a session happy or suicidal. Patient's suicidal thoughts often come from feelings and thoughts of hopelessness. Their lives are so bad and they believe they will never change. Since part of my philosophy of therapy is that people can change, it is not hard for me to try to convince patients that their life can be different. I tend to be very optimistic in my overall philosophy. Confession number eighty-four: I sometimes imagine what would happen if a depressed, pessimistic therapist was honest with a suicidal patient. "Dr. Hopeless, my life is a mess. My wife just left me for another woman, my business is going bankrupt, and my kids hate me. I am just going to kill myself." "Jeff, I know how you feel. I've been there before. It is probably the best thing you could do. Let's problem solve about the quickest and cleanest way to do it."

I just got a quick note from my attorney. What if there really is a Dr. Hopeless somewhere in the world. He will probably sue you for that comment. I wrote my attorney back that Dr. Hopeless would have to take a number and get in line. Tell him to wait right in back of Dr. Shrink.

Some patients use suicidal thoughts and superficial suicide attempts just to get attention. (See my earlier thoughts on borderline personality disorder.) Guess what? It actually works. It is hard not to pay attention to someone with a gun at his or her head. By the way you may want to know what some of my favorite superficial suicide attempts are. I have had a patient cut her wrists with the dull side of the scissors. I have had a patient take a handful of aspirin. Many patients take overdoses of psychiatric medications that they know will not kill them. I have come up with a few additional ideas for superficial suicide attempts. Driving your car at three MPH into a tree. Jumping off a step stool. Spraying ant spray without opening the window. Playing Russian roulette without putting any bullets in the gun. Eating at a certain restaurant in L.A. No, I will not name the restaurant. The line to sue me is already too long.

March 7

It's time for another update on my patients. My first patient is BD. BD only wants to talk about his daughter today. He wants to know how to stop giving money to his daughter. He has funneled about thirty thousand dollars a year to her for the past decade. He wants to know why she isn't more motivated to make it on her own. I try to explain to him that if someone gave me thirty thousand dollars a year for not working I wouldn't have much motivation to work either.

My next patient is FG. FG brings in some of her artwork to show me. She very much wants my approval for her artwork. It doesn't bother her that I know nothing about art. I have a dilemma. If I tell her I like her work she will be happy but I would basically be lying. If I tell her I don't like her work she would be angry with me and tell me she shouldn't practice anymore. If I don't answer her question she will be angry that I am not reinforcing her progress. I try my best to not answer, but finally break down and tell her it's great.

The third patient is NK. NK and I spend the entire session talking about the results of her vocational interest inventory. Here is another great opportunity for my biases to emerge. She scores high on both attorney and schoolteacher interests. I try to convince her that there are enough attorneys in L.A.

The fourth patient is MG, a 17-year-old with mild OCD. She is a dream patient. She does all of her assignments and probably will be done with therapy in a few weeks. I have to convince her today to pray that bad things will happen. Most OCD patients don't like this assignment. They tell me that they will cut out their excessive prayers but do not want to pray for bad things. I had one patient pray that every airplane would crash for two weeks. I think he was a little disappointed to find out that his prayers really didn't have the powers he believed they had. I felt the same way as a kid after watching many Boston Red Sox games and praying for them to win.

I get a break for lunch and then see TN. She actually runs out of things to say after twenty-five minutes. I charge her for a half session and let her go early. I think it would have been more painful for me to sit in silence for the last twenty minutes of the session.

My sixth patient is a new evaluation and is about ten minutes late. I finally realize that someone has again locked the waiting room door from the inside and my patient has been sitting in the hallway for ten minutes. I manage to give the patient the full forty-five minutes and have her fill out all the forms at the end of the session. The patient leaves me a message later that day stating that it was "immoral" for me to charge her for a full session since the reason the session did not start on time was not her fault. Immoral is defined as not in conformity with accepted principles of right and wrong. Confession number eighty-five: I want to call her back and tell her it is immoral for her to accuse me of being immoral since I did give her every minute of the promised time.

My seventh and last patient of the day is ML and it is a phone session. This patient is vacationing in New York so there is a legitimate reason for a phone session. She has some pretty violent obsessions. One of the things I try to convince her of is the fact that these thoughts are just like junk mail. They are really meaningless but you can't prevent them from ever coming into your head. I also tell her that if they are junk she really doesn't need to pay attention to them. I did not tell her that I actually like to look at a lot of my junk mail.

The day is over and I feel pretty good about the work I did. I am actually looking forward to another group of patients my next work day.

March 10

One of my patients today is another therapist. He is a marriage and family therapist who is quite depressed. At one point in the session he looks at me and asks, "Don't you think everything we do is a bunch of crap?" In trying to remain honest with him I tell him that occasionally I do feel that way, but most of the time I feel I am helping people, how else could I be doing this for so long? He replies that maybe I need to believe I am helping people so that I can continue to work.

One of the patients I have told about this book insists on knowing what I said about her. She finds it hard to believe that I have not made fun of any of her problems. I try to tell her that I have used her as an example of a patient who is enjoyable to see because she is so entertaining. She still doesn't believe me. Since she is currently suing her present employer I doubt that I will put anything negative about her in this book.

I get a message today from a patient who wants to know my opinion of her. She wants to know if "she is a normal human being who is just having difficulty coping with a great deal of stress or a worthless piece of shit who doesn't deserve to live." Confession number eighty-six: I want to call her back and tell her I need some time to think about her question.

March 11

I do practice in L.A. and every now and then I get a referral of a famous person. Confession number eighty-seven: I have to admit it boosts my self-esteem to see famous patients. It is sometimes very difficult to sit through a session without asking them about their profession. There is a major problem with seeing famous people: I can't tell any of my friends who my patients are. I have had dinner with friends who continually try to guess the names of my patients. I tell them that even if they guess correctly I will tell them they are wrong. I had one friend actually show up in my waiting room one day to see who my patients were. Breaking patient confidentiality could be very costly. I could be sued and lose my license to practice.

One of my most difficult confidentiality issues occurred a few years ago when I was seeing a patient who started talking about this "asshole" accountant that he worked with. Turned out the "asshole" was one of my best friends. I tried to tell the patient that I knew this person but that did not stop him from ranting and raving about him. I couldn't break confidentiality and tell my friend anything.

Since one of my own interests is sports it would actually be a nightmare for me to see a professional athlete and not talk to him about his sport. How could I see Shaquile O'Neal and not talk to him about his free throw shooting? How could I see Michael Jordan and not get his autograph for my son?

March 13

One of my patients today was telling me about a friend of hers who knew when anyone was not telling her the truth. She said her friend had a bullshit meter. This got me to thinking. Where can I get one of those machines? What a valuable device to have in a therapy session. I would put the meter right across from where the patient sits. Each time the patient is bullshitting me, the meter needle would swing wildly and bells would go off. If a patient told me he had not been able to do his relaxation practice because he couldn't find a cd player, the bullshit meter would ring loudly. If he told me that he forgot his checkbook, so he couldn't pay today, the bullshit meters bells would ring like church bells. If he told me he had to cancel the appointment last week at the last minute because his car broke down, the bullshit meter might actually explode. Confession number eighty-eight: It would be a major concern, though, if the meter also detected any therapist bullshit. It would not be good if a patient asked me if I really believed he could be helped and I replied that he could and then the meter would go wild. It would not be good if I told a the patient that I had no openings next week and the meter started ringing like Big Ben striking twelve. It would not be good for me to tell the patient that therapy will only last about ten weeks and then the meter would start smoking.

Before buying the meter, I would want to see the research behind its development. In order to test the validity of the machine we would need to bring it to a group of people who we already know are bullshitters to make sure that it picks up the bullshit when they talk. I imagine we could use lawyers or politicians for this group. Then, we would also need to look at a group of people who do not bullshit so that we could make sure the meter doesn't generate any false positives. I have narrowed down this group to two-year-olds and golden retrievers.

March 14

I am taking another day off today to get some more of those exciting continuing education units. The lecture today is in Las Vegas. Because I get continuing education units, which makes my entire stay in Las Vegas tax deductible. Instead of staying in the cheap hotel where the talk is located I choose one of the nicer ones. My food, travel and convention fees are all deductible. I do not think my gambling losses are deductible. I actually enjoy one of the speakers and have to hold my head up so that I won't fall asleep for another speaker.

Because I am in private practice I have quite a few business expenses that are deductible. Some of these expenses include magazines for my waiting room, dinners with other therapists or potential referral sources (which could be anyone), a pager, a cell phone and office furniture. I get to buy all my favorite electronic toys like a PDA and a digital camera and use them in my practice. Confession number eighty-nine: I would love to sit in on an IRS audit of a psychologist. "So Dr. Deduction, could you please tell us how you use that vibrating massage chair in your clinical practice? And, can you prove to us that you attended any meetings at that weeklong conference in Maui?" It seems like almost anything could be claimed as a deduction for a therapist. I could attend a workshop on sports psychology given at a tennis resort. I could equip my office with a great sound system to play relaxing music for patients. I could probably hire a personal trainer to teach me about exercise as a way of stress management. However, I am still having difficulty figuring out a way to deduct my son's video game collection.

March 17

I am actually seeing two patients with the same fear: nausea and vomiting. I have already described the most effective treatment for phobias as some type of exposure therapy. I run into a slight problem in attempting to do exposure therapy with this fear. There are many small exposure steps that could be used to help treat these patients. I could have them read about someone vomiting. I could have them watch a movie where someone vomits (although I probably would choose something other than *The Exorcist*). I could have them look at fake vomit (another important prop that a therapist always has in his desk). I could have them eat foods that they have been avoiding (although some foods might also make me nauseous). Additionally, some behavior therapists have created their own recipes for vomit to use for exposures. My favorite one consists of combining beef barley soup, cream of mushroom soup, blue cheese or other crumbly, strong smelling cheese and then adding oatmeal flakes to achieve the desired consistency. The mixture is sealed and left in a clear container in the sun for a few days. This works very well in exposing the patient to vomit, but how do you expose someone to actually vomiting for the sake of practice? There is a drug, ipecac, which is used to purposely induce vomiting. I have had many patients with this fear and not one has agreed to take ipecac as a final test of the effectiveness of the treatment. Confession number ninety: If a patient agreed to take the ipecac I would not schedule the exposure in my office.

Truth be told there are actually other common fears that tend to be difficult to implement exposures for. Many patients have a fear of death. I can take them to a cemetery. I can have them read obituaries. I can have them watch movies about people dying. However, the patient will only be able to truly expose himself to his ultimate fear one time.

I received a call today from an attorney. He has a client who worked at a crematorium but did not cremate the bodies; he let them just "stack up." I asked the attorney how I could help him. He wanted to know if his client is appropriate for the UCLA OCD program. I told him that I am a bit confused. What does this have to do with OCD? The attorney then asked me if his client's problem is hoarding. After I regain my ability to speak, I told him that I think this is not hoarding.

March 18

I had to complete an application today for re-certification of my staff privileges at the UCLA Neuropsychiatric Hospital. It is a rather routine application that includes "attestation questions." These are questions aimed at gathering information about anything unethical or illegal that you have done since the last time you filled out the form. One of my favorite questions is, "Do you presently use drugs illegally?" Can you imagine the IQ of anyone who answers this question "yes?" My guess is that these questions are for the legal defense of the hospital. When someone is charged with some heinous crime while on drugs the hospital can say, "Well, he swore that he wasn't using drugs illegally."

There are other questions on the form that ask you if you are capable of performing all of your duties. Confession number ninety-one: I would love to write on the form that I am reapplying for clinical privileges. However, I am totally incompetent. Maybe I will write that after I am sure I am retiring. Does anybody actually read these forms?

There are also questions about one's mental stability. I wonder if you would be denied privileges to a psychiatric hospital on the basis of having a psychiatric disorder. I imagine receiving a letter back from the hospital: "Dr. Tarlow, we have carefully reviewed your application for recertification and regretfully have to deny your privileges. Your previous history of being depressed for two days in 1974 is the reason for the denial. We are basing this evidence on the recent article in the *Journal of Insignificant Results*, which warns that previous episodes of depression may be contagious. We encourage you to reapply in ten years."

There are also questions involving various crimes that you may have committed since the last application. I wonder what crimes are permitted in order to continue practicing. I would imagine murder, assault, and armed robbery are no-nos. But what about nice white-collar crimes like tax fraud? I purposely did not tell them about my traffic violation for rolling through a stop sign.

After completing my application I realize that I am squeaky clean. Not only should I be able to be recertified, I might be able to run for political office.

March 20

I actually have three new evaluations today. Many therapists like to take a few sessions to evaluate patients. Given the nature of my personality I like to be able to make a diagnosis in the first two minutes. Confession number ninety-two: I have had a fantasy of being called to participate in a new television quiz show called "Speed Diagnosis." I picture three professionals as contestants: a psychiatrist, a social worker, and myself. They bring in a patient to interview. You then try to determine who can make the fastest correct diagnosis. As soon as you know the diagnosis you hit the buzzer. You could even get extra points for making a diagnosis without even asking questions. For example, some patients may look so depressed that you don't even have to ask questions.

One of the evaluations today is a referral from a psychiatrist who wants me to give a second opinion regarding the diagnosis and treatment of one of her patients. A request for a second opinion means the patient has not improved and the treating professional is not sure what to do. This case turns out to be unlike any that I have ever seen. The patient is a forty-five-year-old married female who is having very clear-cut aggressive obsessions. Although she doesn't want to harm herself she is afraid that she will do very self-destructive acts. For example, she is afraid that she will take a knife from the drawer and stab herself. I have seen many patients with similar thoughts. What makes this person different is that she actually takes the knife out of the drawer and presses it against her to see how far she will go. OCD patients never do this! They are generally so afraid of the behavior that they throw out all the knives in their house. This person continually "tests" the limits with all of her thoughts. It reminds me somewhat of the old movie *Harold and Maude*. Harold continually tests the limits of how to kill himself in the movie.

By the end of the evaluation I am thoroughly convinced of one thing. I do not want this person for a patient. I call the referring psychiatrist and tell her I concur with her treatment and wish her luck.

March 21

I generally do not see many patients with a diagnosis of bipolar disorder. Bipolar disorder is the current name for manic-depressive disorder. Occasionally I get a referral of a patient who has bipolar disorder and wants help in controlling the depressions that occur as part of the disorder. Most of these patients have a history of at least one manic episode, but are not currently manic. However, there are times that one of these patients cycles into a manic episode during the course of my treatment. There are of course different levels of manic behavior. Milder symptoms of mania are often referred to as hypomania. One of the symptoms of hypomania is that the patient is extremely talkative. Today I have a patient in my office who is hypomanic. As he enters the session he starts to talk. It is virtually impossible to interrupt him. Confession number ninety-three: I have this thought of trying to sneak out of the office while he is talking, go get a snack, say hello to some of my colleagues and then re-enter my office. I picture the patient just continuing to talk while I am gone and continuing to talk without a break as I re-enter the office.

Another symptom that often occurs during hypomania is that the patient's thoughts are tangential. This means that the patient generally transitions from one topic to another topic that does not appear to be related to the first topic. When patients have done this I often find myself scratching my head. How did he get to that? What does that have to do with what he was just talking about? If I spend too much time trying to answer these questions to myself the patient will probably be talking about something else.

Since I tend to be very directive in my therapy sessions I find it quite difficult to work with manic patients. Even if I try to get them on task, I often lose. At that point I try to sit back, listen, fantasize about being somewhere else and wait for the session to end.

March 24

A few patients today want to talk politics. The United States has many troops in the Middle East. The patients really don't want to talk about how the war affects them. It appears they just want to convince me of their positions on the war. I politely listen to their views and then try to get them to believe I am one of the good guys. I really believe that they would terminate treatment if they found out that my position was one hundred and eighty degrees opposite of theirs.

After a long day at work I come home to get a little bit of relaxation. I decide to watch the TV show *The Practice*. About halfway through the show, one of the lead characters consults a therapist to talk about some of the problems he has been having with his wife. The therapist seems to be making some very interesting interpretations when I notice he starts to wrinkle up his nose. In the next two minutes the therapist repeats this behavior about ten times. Now, this is supposed to be a serious show. I understood when David Kelly, the writer of this show and the show *Alley McBeal*, portrayed some of Alley's therapists as "unusual." In fact, my favorite portrayal of a therapist was when Alley's therapist put on music and started to dance during the session. After seeing this latest portrayal of a therapist, I might guess that Mr. Kelly has not had very positive experiences with his own therapists.

I am sure that by now some of you want to know if I have ever been in therapy. Confession number ninety-four: I have only had about fifteen sessions of therapy as a patient in my life. One period of five sessions occurred when I was having difficulty in a relationship. Shortly after the therapy ended I broke off the relationship. The other ten sessions occurred right after a girl friend dumped me in 1978. I must say that it felt awfully good to not have to listen to the therapist's problems. However, I have not been in therapy since then. I prefer to save my money for my annual Hawaii trip.

March 25

I have a patient today who is having the sexual problem of premature ejaculation. He is not currently in a relationship and is petrified to enter a relationship because he feels that a woman would reject him if this problem occurred. In the past, I have a treated a number of patients with this problem who were currently involved in relationships. If that happens I generally bring the spouse into the sessions to aid the treatment. On several occasions, this being one, there was no woman available to help the patient. This is when I turn to the aid of a sexual surrogate. These women are actually certified by an organization to work with patients who are having sexual problems. They are not prostitutes, and some of them are actually studying psychology in school. Most patients want to interview several of the surrogates and choose the one that they feel they could "work" best with. Most of the surrogates are older women who have been doing this work for a long time. Many psychologists are reluctant to use surrogates because of legal and ethical issues. Since my patients have had such positive experiences with surrogates, I don't have a problem recommending them to a patient.

Each week the patient returns to therapy and tells me about his session with the sexual surrogate. As the sessions progress the descriptions become more and more "x-rated." Confession number ninety-five: At this point in his treatment I try to schedule the patient for a late afternoon session. I know his descriptions of the surrogate sessions will keep me awake.

March 27

At long last the building management in Calabasas has told me that construction on the improvements in my office suite will start today! They inform me that all loud construction will be done outside of normal business hours. The construction crew arrives an hour late to begin the process. The only problem is that I have patients scheduled the entire morning and the construction noise is horrific. At times the entire room feels like an amusement park ride. I am grateful that I do not have any relaxation training scheduled. It is unfortunate that I don't have any patients who are afraid of turbulence. I could just tell them that the session was a planned exposure.

The construction crew tells me that it is not in the plans to put sound insulation in the new walls. I try to explain to them that it is not in my plans to be able to hear everything another therapist and patient are saying. The very first private practice office I ever rented had the worst soundproofing of any therapist office I have ever seen. Confession number ninety-six: When patients in the next office began to sob loudly, I had this urge to run next door and hand them some Kleenex.

My office suite will have three separate offices when the construction is done. That means three therapists could be seeing patients at the same time. Or, if I wanted to use the dentist model, I could see three different patients at the same time. I could work with one patient for a few minutes, give her an assignment, and tell her I will be back to check on her in a few minutes, and then dash into the next office to work with a different patient. To my knowledge this technique has not been tried as yet by any therapist. If it were to be attempted I am sure that Southern California would be the place to start.

March 28

I purposely scheduled a day off today. Although I did not see any patients I did return a number of patient calls. In the evening my wife and I had dinner with another psychologist and her husband who is not a psychologist. As the three psychologists talked "shop," I wondered what it might be like to be in his position. Is the conversation boring?

Does he believe that by virtue of being married to a psychologist for a number of years that he is able to do therapy himself? I decided to ask him these questions. His wife said he would actually be a very directive therapist. The type of therapist that just tells you to stop whining and get over it. Confession number ninety-seven: I think he might be a better therapist than about fifty percent of the real ones. His directive approach may actually be refreshing.

March 31

Once again I find myself in a theoretical/ethical dilemma with one of my patients. A patient begins to tell me about his problems in deciding what type of car to get his sixteen- year old. I have no problem agreeing with him that a BMW would be inappropriate for his son's first car. He then tells me that his son would really like a convertible and that no one in his or her right mind would drive a convertible. He looks for my reaction and I am silent. However, it appears that I have not completely hidden my feelings. He asks: "You don't drive a convertible do you?" I again remain silent and he says: "You do, don't you?" I refuse to lie to this patient. I tell him I do drive a convertible and I feel it is safe. The patient feels bad thinking he has just insulted me. I think next time I will just lie and tell a patient what they really want to hear.

One of my patients today asks me if it is okay to take notes during the session. I tell him it is okay to take notes or even to record the session. However, I inform him, if he sells the tapes I expect some royalties. Confession number ninety-eight: Maybe I could put together an album. "The Best of Gerald Tarlow, Ph.D." I could record all my sessions, choose the most entertaining and put them together in one album. I now have a project to start on as soon as I finish this book.

Later in the day a twenty-seven-year-old patient tells me that she is afraid that she is becoming a "butt monkey." I wonder if I am really that out of touch with her generation. It is a phrase I have never heard before. Do I ask her what it means or just give it a good educated guess? I decide to ask her and I am informed that it is similar to being a slave or lackey. I can't wait to get home and use the expression with my teenage son the next time he asks me if I can get him something from the refrigerator.

CHAPTER 7
April

April 1

Today is April Fool's Day, a very important day for anyone with a sense of humor. Confession number ninety-nine: Every year I think of all the clever April Fool's jokes I could play on my patients and every year I never follow through with these jokes. Let's start with my answering machine message. I have thought about changing my outgoing message to: "You have reached the office of Dr. Gerald Tarlow. He is no longer in practice. However, if it would make you feel better you can make an appointment after the tone." I thought about telling some patients that I was retiring because of them. I thought of telling others that I have decided to shorten the sessions to fifteen minutes and please talk fast. I thought of pretending to fall asleep during the session. Maybe I could ask the patient to hold his or her thought for a minute while I make a phone call and pretend to order some food for lunch.

I have thought about starting the session with: "the first thing I want to talk about today is the Boston Red Sox. What do you think their chances are of winning the World Series this year?" I thought about bringing in a friend of mine who is a comedian and having him greet my patients at the door. "I'm sorry, Dr. Tarlow is ill today. I am the substitute therapist." I have thought of dressing differently, either wearing a suit and tie or shorts and sandals. How about the old whoopee cushion. I think I could get good reactions from either placing it under my chair or the patient's chair. There are just so many possibilities. In the end I chicken out and I do not play any April Fool's jokes on any of my patients. However, friends and family are fair game.

April 3

Every few months licensed psychologists in California receive a newsletter from the Board of Psychology in Sacramento. The newsletter discusses new laws that affect psychologists, new course requirements for continuing education, and helpful hints for private practioners. Confession number 100: My favorite section of the newsletter is the "Disciplinary Actions." In this section we get to find out all the bad things other psychologists have done to either lose their license or be put on probation. I believe probation means you can continue to practice but are not allowed to answer your phone during a session. The psychologists mentioned in the disciplinary actions are identified by name. In the current newsletter eight psychologists were put on probation and five psychologists had their license revoked or voluntarily surrendered their license. Here are some of the recent reasons for disciplinary actions:

1. Dishonest, corrupt or fraudulent act.
   Functioning outside field of competence.
   Repeated negligent acts.

2. Act of sexual relations with a patient.

3. Sexual exploitation.

4. Conviction of a crime substantially
   related to the practice of psychology.

5. Fraudulently or neglectfully misrepresenting the
   type of status of license or registration actually held.

6. Use of a controlled substance or
   alcohol in a dangerous manner.

If the Board is going to give us this much information, I think they might as well supply all the details. For example, did the psychologist pass himself off as an attorney, an FBI agent or maybe just a psychiatrist? How far did the psychologist's sexual relationship go? Did he just get to first base or did he hit a home run? What controlled substance did the psychologist take? Was it just some marijuana or is he a heroin addict? By the way, if the psychologist had used the marijuana in a non-dangerous way, would he still have gotten in trouble? How many negligent acts were repeated? It would be interesting to know if the psychologist had gotten away with 374 negligent acts before he was caught. What type of crime did the psychologist commit related to the practice of psychology? My guess is that he shoplifted a self-help book from the bookstore. Or maybe he just stole some food to give to an anorexic patient. After all, inquiring minds want to know.

I also want to know what happens if you are a friend or acquaintance of one of these psychologists. I can imagine running into one of them that I know. "Hey, Bruce, I just read about you in the Board of Psychology newsletter. How's the new job at McDonalds?" I think if it were me I would move someplace where no one knew me and never mention the fact that I was a psychologist.

April 4

It is one of those days when my job is to listen to people whine and complain. I don't really think my patients today want to learn to change anything. One patient complains about how he is being harassed on his job, how uncomfortable it is to work there and could I please get him off work because of excessive stress. Another couple comes in to complain about their son who doesn't want to talk to them and doesn't want help. I am apparently the tenth therapist they have gone to and their son is still the same. Another patient wants to complain about his in-laws. I thought you could just do that with your friends. I didn't think you needed a psychologist for that type of complaining. A final patient whines and complains about everything in her life. She can't find a job. She doesn't have any friends. She is broke. Her favorite TV show is being cancelled and Baskin-Robbins just put her favorite ice cream on vacation.

I do a great job of listening to these complaints and trying to be supportive. Most of my suggestions tend to be ignored. I have read that in ancient times there was a person whose role it was to absorb all of the angst of anyone in the city. The person was a vessel for angst. I wondered, where does this person go when his vessel is full? I know that I had to go home to have dinner with my wife and son. That was very unfortunate for them. If my son complained about anything that night he was in big trouble. It didn't matter if the complaint was valid. "Hey dad, the light in the twenty foot high ceiling is burnt out and I can't replace the bulb." "Son, I think we will just have to wait until you are tall enough to replace it." If I were my family I would probably call me before the end of each day. "How was your day? Did you feel like you accomplished anything today? Is your vessel full?" If I answer yes to the last question they should probably just pack their bags and leave a note for me to read when I get home. "Dear Jerry, on your way home we were called by a radio station and won an immediate trip for two to a secret resort for the weekend. Since you were not home yet, the two of us went without you. We will try to contact you when we find out where they are taking us. If you don't hear from us, I am sure we will see you on Monday. Please don't abuse the dog while we are gone."

Confession number 101: I feel that I only have one excellent outlet for my own frustration and anger: sports. I play a great deal of tennis and I do get angry on the tennis court. I have always justified the anger by saying that I can't yell at my patients or at my wife and kid. If I break a tennis racquet or two it may be cheaper than years of psychotherapy. Watching sports and yelling at the players on the TV screen also helps. I sometimes feel that if I yell loud enough at them they might just hear me in New York.

April 7

I had a new patient scheduled for five p.m. today. He never showed up and never called to cancel the appointment. I left him a message at about 5:25 p.m. telling him that he had a five o'clock appointment and asking him to call me back to let me know what happened. He never called to apologize or give me an excuse for why he didn't show up. How rude, self centered and inconsiderate some people are. I obviously can't bill him for the time since I had never seen him previously. It is one of the things that occur in my practice that makes me angry. I wonder what the patient is thinking. "I'm sure Dr. Tarlow has plenty of other patients in his waiting room. It doesn't matter if one of them doesn't show up." Confession number 102: If this patient ever calls back to set up another appointment, I think that I will not mention this incident. I'll just schedule an appointment for a Wednesday when I am not in the office. I'll let him show up for the appointment and sit in my waiting room for an hour before he realizes that I am not there. When he calls to yell at me for not being there, I could just tell him I did the same thing he did to me.

I wonder what makes other therapists angry. What is the most unpleasant part of the job? I've decided to take an informal survey. I have left messages for some of my colleagues asking them this question. One psychologist told me that the thing that makes her the angriest is a patient who cancels at the last minute after she has rearranged her entire schedule to give a patient an appointment for a time when the therapist is not normally working. Another therapist told me that talking to patients at times when he has no desire to talk to them makes him angry. For example, a patient leaving an urgent message to call him when the therapist is in the middle of playing a tennis match.

April 8

For the first time in a long time I had a patient decide to lie down on my couch as if she were in analysis. I found this interesting. I did not have to make eye contact with her. I could actually close my eyes and nap while she was talking. Confession number 103: I had a strong desire to make an interpretation about the patient's toilet training. I did resist, but I definitely would have liked to see if my interpretation was accepted. I have a couch, a recliner, and my desk chair in my office. Most patients generally ask me where they should sit at the beginning of the first session. I generally tell them it is okay to sit anywhere except for the desk chair. In all my years of practice I have had only one patient who then sat in my chair. I think she may have had control issues. About fifty percent of the patients sit on the end of the couch nearest to my chair, and thirty percent sit in the recliner. Only a few patients use the reclining feature of the chair. Twenty percent sit on the couch as far away from me as possible. Generally, most of these patients are women.

One of my patients calls me and tells me he is going to be twenty to twenty five minutes late, but he will be at the session. He arrives at exactly thirty-seven minutes past the hour giving me time for an eight-minute session. I talk very rapidly and actually feel that I have accomplished something with this patient in eight minutes. I think to myself that I could get about six of these eight-minute sessions into an hour. A very famous old book about doing psychotherapy was entitled *The Fifty Minute Hour*. I could do the new millennium edition entitled *The Eight Minute Hour*. I believe this approach might be very helpful for the busy business executive under a great deal of time pressure.

April 10

I have two patients today who are very close to finishing therapy. The first is a fear of flying patient who has completed five sessions of Virtual Reality Therapy. She has actually scheduled a flight for the end of the month and another one for May. The VR technique continues to amaze me in terms of its effectiveness. I really believe many more people could be helped if my partner and I wanted to invest in marketing the treatment. This is another one of those tasks that psychologists are just not trained for. Let's consider the possibilities: (1) we could send a junk mail flyer to everyone in the surrounding area. (2) We could send a junk e-mail to everyone in the world. (3) We could start an 800 number similar to 1-800-DENTIST. Such as 1-800-GETONAPLANE. (4) We could have successful patients give testimonials to the local press. "Dr. Tarlow saved my marriage by helping me overcome my fear of flying." (5) We could do a radio ad either during a travel talk show or self-help talk show. And (6) we could do a television ad. I can't decide whether I should be the spokesman on the television ad or should hire someone like Tom Cruise who patients might mistakenly think was me.

The second patient has been able to eliminate many of his obsessive thoughts. He has done a great job in doing the therapy homework. He was able to complete treatment in about ten sessions. Confession number 104: I am getting concerned that patients are getting better too fast. My waiting list is shrinking and mental health is becoming desirable.

April 11

Incredibly, I finish the week the same way I started it: another patient does not show up for his first appointment. However, this one is even worse than the one on Monday. I had just confirmed the appointment with this patient yesterday. If he calls back I will schedule him for the same time as the other no-show. They both could be sitting around in my waiting room waiting for me to not show up.

I also got a call today from an old patient that I saw about eight years ago. The patient told me how much I had helped him and wanted to know if I had time to see him again. Lucky for me I remembered that this was a patient from hell. Confession number 105: Any time I do not want to see a patient I tell the patient that I have a very long waiting list. "I'm sorry Jim, I have a waiting list that is about four years long. I would be happy to add your name to the list." This strategy generally works. Occasionally there is a patient who tells me to go ahead and add his name to the waiting list. Sometimes these patients even call back. "Dr. Tarlow, it's been four-and-a-half years. Where am I on the waiting list now?"

One of my patients today informs me that according to feng shui, my office is set up all wrong. I immediately got up from my desk chair and sat on the couch hoping to get into a better feng shui therapy position. The patient did not find this very humorous and insisted that I return to the desk chair. I make a mental note to not try any practical jokes on this patient next April Fool's day.

April 13

My first patient today was a woman who told me in the previous session that she was going to take a course on overcoming procrastination. I made a note of it and made sure to ask her about the course today. When she told me that she hadn't made it to the course I almost spit out the water I had in my mouth.

At times patients wear some very strange clothes. Today one of my patients wore a shirt that I believe used to belong to a circus clown. Another patient wore pants that were so shiny I had to put sunglasses on. I have had patients dress as though they were about to go to bed in their favorite pajamas and other patients dress like they were going to a formal ball. What is the proper patient attire? Confession number 106: I think that patients should dress according to their disorder. This would make it easier for the psychologist to diagnose the patient. Depressed patients should only wear black. Obsessive compulsive patients should have striped shirts that line up with striped pants. People addicted to marijuana should wear tie dyed shirts and bell-bottom jeans. Paranoid patients should wear sunglasses and a hat covering their face. Patients with insomnia should definitely wear pajamas.

There are times when patients do wear sunglasses during the session. This is very disturbing since I can't see their eyes and I therefore do not know when I have an opportunity to yawn during the session. Whenever a patient does this maybe I should just put my sunglasses on and ask the patient if the ever saw the movie *Blues Brothers*.

April 15

One of my patients today asked me if I would like to adopt her 16 year-old daughter whom she was having difficulty communicating with. I asked her if she would just like to trade her for my teenage son and call it even.

I have run into a major problem in being a psychologist. Every year the school system has a day when you take your son to work with you. It is an opportunity for fathers to show their sons what they do every day. This has been fairly difficult in my job. Let's imagine for a minute that I do get all of my patients that day to give permission for my son to be in the session with us. Since my son does not particularly like to listen, as soon as a patient started talking he would probably interrupt the patient and start asking questions. He also would tend to do very directive therapy. "What do you mean you are afraid to fly? I've been flying since I was six months old. It's no big deal." He also would be very direct when a patient is not logical. "How can anyone be afraid of clowns? They aren't going to hurt you!" Confession number 107: Now that I think of it, some of my patients probably would benefit from a session or two with him.

April 17

In preparing for my upcoming vacation, I purchased some new headphones so that I could listen to music on the plane. The headphones are noise-canceling and help to drown out the engine noise on the plane. Confession number 108: I have this urge to try them out for a few select patients during therapy sessions. I could tell the patients that I was researching a new treatment technique and wanted to see if it would be effective for their problem. I could put the headphones on, and continue to shake my head up and down, but not hear anything the patient was saying.

I have always been interested in evaluating new therapeutic techniques that might help patients. I often find that when a new "hot" technique is discovered there are therapists who want to apply the technique to every psychological problem. One such technique is EMDR. EMDR stands for eye movement desensitization and reprocessing. It is a technique discovered about twenty years ago by a psychologist. The technique was originally used for patients suffering post-traumatic stress disorder (PTSD). It consisted of patients retelling their "trauma" while tracking the back and forth movement of the therapist's finger in front of their eyes. Although the technique was originally very controversial, a number of good research studies showed that it was effective for PTSD. This result led to some practitioners using the technique for any psychological disorder. You have panic attacks? Let's try EMDR. How about obsessive-compulsive disorder? Let's try EMDR. You say you have a bad eating disorder. Have you tried EMDR? Confession number 109: I am waiting for the infomercial with testimonials from patients recently discharged from a psychiatric hospital stating; "My life was a mess. I lost my job, my wife left me, and I wanted to kill myself. Then I went to Dr. I Mvmt and had two sessions of EMDR. I just married a super model and won the lottery. I owe everything to EMDR."

April 18

Today I received some more responses to my psychologist survey of what makes therapists angry. One psychologist told me that the worst thing he could think of was the need to diplomatically tell a patient: "You are being a complete fucking idiot!" The final respondent told me that it was "being bored by boring clients with the same boring disorders." This is truly a double whammy. A boring patient with a boring disorder.

I received a brochure in the mail today for an upcoming continuing education class titled "The Impossible Patient." The brochure listed several learning objectives of the course including: (1) to understand the key difficulties between dimensional and categorical approaches to personality disorders. (2) To describe the diagnostic criteria and clinical clues for assessing personality disorders. (3) To list both general and specific guidelines for effective treatment of patients diagnosed with a personality disorder. And (4) to discuss potential sources of patient non-compliance and how these may be addressed by the clinician. Confession number 110: These would not be my objectives with an impossible patient. My goals for educating clinicians would include: (1) how to transfer your patient to an unsuspecting colleague. (2) How to prevent the patient from filing multiple lawsuits against you. (3) How to believe the statement "I can't help everyone. And (4) how to avoid beating your wife and kids after meeting with the patient.

April 19

It is my first day of vacation. I am vacationing in Maui, probably the most relaxing and stress-reducing vacation of the year. It is a place I frequently tell many of my anxious patients to visit - but not when I am there.

I think when a plastic surgeon goes on vacation that it is probably impossible for him to look at people without thinking about what type of surgery they need. For example, "look at that guy over there. He sure could benefit from a nose job. That woman's thighs are just shouting out for liposuction." Confession number 111: I have discovered that just like the plastic surgeon I cannot escape patients when I am on vacation. I can't help diagnosing certain blatant behaviors that I see. For example, spending time on the beach I can clearly see whether a woman wearing a bathing suit is anorexic. I walk by one of these women today and had a strong urge to whisper "anorexia" out of the side of my mouth. I think if I were anorexic I would at least try to disguise it by wearing a ski jacket.

Later in the day I am trying to relax on the beach and a mother screams at her kid and then spanks him. I think to myself, child abuse waiting to happen.

At night I go to a nice restaurant for dinner and have to use the bathroom. As the person before me finishes in the urinal he flushes it with his foot, takes a paper towel to turn on the faucet in the sink and uses another paper towel to open the bathroom door in leaving the restroom. Bingo, OCD. I have such a strong urge to hand him my card, but I refrain.

I realize it is probably unrealistic for me to truly get a vacation from my profession.

April 25

It is my first day back from vacation and it seems that most of my patients today are attorneys. There seems to be an unusually high percentage of my patients who are attorneys. I can only guess at some of the reasons this is so. Most of the attorneys work for large law firms and seem to work twelve to fourteen-hour days, six or seven days per week. This schedule would seem to lend itself to excess stress, insomnia, depression, and poor interpersonal relationships, especially with a spouse. Although most of these attorneys are in dire need of psychotherapy, few of them have the time to schedule regular appointments. Many of them have a habit of canceling their appointments on short notice, but always paying for the session. Confession number 112: I think these big law firms should employ in house shrinks. First, it would save the employee time. Instead of spending an extra thirty to sixty minutes commuting to a therapist's office, the employee could just shuffle down the hall and be there in a minute. Another advantage would be that they could employ a therapist specializing in psychological disorders of attorneys. The therapist would know all of the pressures the employee was experiencing. Third, think of all the money the firm would save by not having employees go out on stress leave or sick leave. Now, the only problem would be how to convince a therapist to be part of this "toxic" environment. I guess if you paid a therapist the same salary as the attorneys you could find someone to do it.

April 26

It is time to rent another movie with a therapist in one of the lead roles: *Anger Management.* If you have never been in therapy I am pretty sure you would never want to be after watching this movie. The therapist in this movie actually moves in with his patient, sleeps in the same bed with his patient and goes to work with his patient. For thirty days he is going to be with his patient 24 hours per day. No fee is ever mentioned in the movie, but I have calculated the fee based on a reasonable $200-per-hour rate. The one-month fee comes out to $144,000. I wondered if the patient submitted the bill to his insurance company.

As absurd as the premise of this movie sounds, there are actually stories of patients employing twenty-four-hour-per day therapists. The most infamous one involved Brian Wilson of the Beach Boys and his therapist, Dr. Eugene Landy. The therapist did eventually surrender his license to practice psychology and has been denied reinstatement.

The therapist in the movie also has some unique techniques to help his patients. One of the techniques involves having his patients sing the song "I feel pretty" whenever they get angry. Confession number 113: I am anxiously waiting for this technique to be tried by a real psychologist. Given the power of Hollywood, I would guess that some therapist would actually try this with his patients. I would also guess that this therapist would then be flooded with new referrals.

One of the interesting aspects of the movie is the fact that anger management is a legitimate type of therapy. Angry people tend to be very difficult to treat since most of them do not want therapy. Some are court ordered into therapy. Some are given an ultimatum by their spouse or employer. In fact, they are generally angry about being forced into therapy. Most of the anger problems I have treated are so entrenched in the patient's personality that they are quite difficult to change.

April 28

I received a letter today from the Board of Psychology. I knew I had renewed my license in January and technically there should be no reason for the Board to contact me. Getting a letter from the Board of Psychology is similar to getting a letter from the IRS. Who is suing me? Who is complaining about me? I really don't want to open the letter. However, if I don't open the letter there is no way I can concentrate on any of my patients. It turns out that the letter is an invitation to participate in the process of creating the California Jurisprudence and Professional Ethics Examination. This exam is the final part of the licensing process for new psychologists in California. I have always secretly wanted to be involved in the process of licensing new psychologists but have previously never had the chance. I would love to do my best to prevent many potential bad therapists from ever practicing in California. Confession number 114: I need to participate before this book is published. This book may turn out to be a primer for finding unethical practices in psychology. It may be similar to those picture puzzles that ask you to find the thirty-six rabbits hidden in the picture. "Class, I would like you to read Dr. Tarlow's book and find the 463 violations of the ethics code that he may have committed."

The licensing exam in psychology is not nearly as rigorous as it used to be. Currently there is a national multiple-choice exam followed by a multiple choice ethics exam. A few years ago, the oral exam was eliminated because of the inability to be able to score it objectively. This is actually a shame since the oral exam had an extremely high fail rate. I remember quite clearly my oral exam. One of the questions the examiners asked me was to tell them the areas in which I had the least experience. I truthfully told them that I had little experience working with children or minorities. They then proceeded to ask me how I would treat an Hispanic child. After the examiners picked me up off the floor I proceeded to improvise my way through the question. I realized after the exam that I should have told them I had never worked with adults with anxiety problems. At the end of the exam they asked me if there was anything I wanted to say. I told them that I thought it would have been better if they had asked me about what I said I was going to do, not what I would not do. They informed me that the exam was "generic" and I was required to know everything. I left the room thinking I had failed.

Even though the examiners could have told me at the end of the exam whether I had passed or failed, it took four weeks to get the results of my oral exam back. I truly was surprised to find out I had passed. I personally know some of the best psychologists in L.A. who have failed the exam.

If you failed the exam and wanted to appeal the result, you had to file a formal appeal with the Board of Psychology. Guess what happened if you won the appeal? They did not change the result to a passing score. They allowed you to take the exam over again a few months earlier than the next scheduled exam. Do you think the Board of Psychology may have wanted to limit the appeal process?

April 29

I have another new patient today. He has a rare form of OCD - music in his head that he cannot get rid of. Now I know most people have occasionally heard a song and had that song in their head for a day or two. But with OCD, the song or music becomes the foreground and is nearly impossible to turn off. This is one problem area that non-psychologists are happy to discuss with me. In fact, I have decided to do another survey to try to help me with this patient. I left messages for five of my closest non-psychologist friends to see how they would treat this patient. Everybody likes to pretend they are therapists once in a while. Many people think it is an easy job. Here are the responses to the survey: (1) Get your patient to change the channel to sports talk. (2) Doesn't she have a volume control? (3) Is her music commercial free? (4) If it were my house I would be grateful so that I didn't have to listen to those screaming kids. And (5) from an attorney friend, has she considered suing the radio station? I will take these suggestions under consideration.

It turns out that I had many enjoyable therapy sessions today. Almost every patient wanted to talk about my trip to Hawaii and/or the NBA playoffs. Confession number 115: I should pay my patients to talk about these things. It is pleasurable to think about my recent trip and sports are probably my biggest non-work interest. Perhaps the next time I am feeling depressed I should just go into a travel agency and talk to them for forty-five minutes or call a sports talk radio show. With most of my patients I tend to feel guilty talking about these subjects for more than ten minutes. I then try to get them to talk about their psychological issues.

CHAPTER 8
May

May 1

I think it is time for an update on some of my patients. TH continues to make no progress in treatment, but still enjoys coming into the sessions. She doesn't even talk about her fear of elevators anymore. After obtaining her law degree and passing the bar exam she has now discovered she is miserable being an attorney. Confession number 116: There have been way too many times in my professional career that I wanted to say "I told you so" but never did. We spend today's session talking about what other jobs she could possibly try.

BD continues to be concerned about the psychological and physical state of her daughter. She continues to complain about her marriage and her husband. I continue to listen. One of the pleasant things about BD is that she often tells me a joke at the end of the session. It is a very pleasant way to end sessions.

NK has been progressing nicely. She continues to investigate new jobs and has been making progress on making other decisions. She has been trying very hard to buy a car. Since I have had excellent continuing education classes on this subject from Consumer Reports, I am able to give her some direct advice.

MW does not come to the session with his mother. However, he has decided to become a certified hypnotherapist. Although he is enjoying the classes, this is a big mistake. He is attending a hypnosis school in L.A. I believe the qualifications for admission are the ability to pay tuition and get to the classes. I try to picture MW doing hypnosis with a client. One of his symptoms was that he had to repeat things until they were perfect. "Okay, I want you to close your eye. No, I want you to close your eyes. No, I want you to shut your eyes. No, please close your eyes. No, please shut your eyes...."

It is NH's last session today. She is ready to graduate from therapy. She has made considerable improvement in her OCD, but it will never be 100 percent gone. It is extremely rewarding for me to see her get better and to be able to do things she couldn't do six months ago. When a patient completes treatment I try to tell them that they were responsible for getting better, not me. However, I do know that I helped the process and that they probably would have been in therapy for another few years with some other therapists.

FG continues to have her ups and downs each week. I can never predict her mood from one week to the next. At some sessions she is so positive and optimistic, and at other sessions I feel that I should be wearing full body armor to protect myself. I think about asking her to call me the morning of the session to warn me about her mood.

May 2

I am doing marital therapy today with a couple. I ask them about their goals in treatment. One of the first issues that come up is how to get one of them to stop yelling at their son. Okay, I just found an issue I really do not like to deal with. I think it is a little too close to home. Confession number 117: I imagine coming home and my teenage son asking me about the patients I saw today. After telling him about how I helped this couple deal with yelling at their son, I imagine him looking at me and saying: "Do you mind if I get some advice from Mike Tyson on how to control my temper?" The couple wants to know if I ever yell at my son. After contemplating the question for a minute I tell them that it does occur on rare occasions. I think I would lose all my therapeutic credibility if I told them that I only yell on days that end in "Y."

It is a problem area that I think I know how to handle from my education. I wonder why I have such difficulty putting my suggestions to this couple into practice for myself. I know the suggestions would work for me as well as it does for my patients. I do believe that we all have a breaking point for anger. How many times can you have someone poke you in the side without getting angry and starting to yell? Some people can take more pokes than others.

I ask the couple what triggers the anger. I discover that the anger often occurs after the wife sees the child's room that looks like it was just hit with a hurricane. Oh no, this is just too much. Has this couple been sent here by my wife to make me feel guilty? Are they just actors who are here to help me with my problems? Or is it just karma? It is hard for a true behaviorist to believe in karma. They want to know how I get my son to clean up his room. I want to tell them that every three months I go into his room with an industrial strength vacuum cleaner and just suck up everything.

May 5

I received a flyer in the mail today advertising "Glass Art aimed towards the Psychological Field." There are pictures of ten of the pieces on a separate page. Four of the pictures are of two naked people embracing. There is a piece of a body of a man with a penis, and other pieces suggesting erotic images. I wonder what therapist in his right mind would display these in his office. They certainly would be conversation pieces if patients ran out of things to say. The only time I ever displayed something that I really wanted patients to talk about was when I purchased the *Pop Up Book of Phobias*. Almost every patient wanted to look through the pictures.

My offices are decorated fairly conservatively. In one office there are two pictures on the walls. Behind the sofa on which most patients sit is a large photograph of Lake Tahoe that I took about twenty years ago. Confession number 118: This photograph is mainly for me. Lake Tahoe is one of my favorite places in the world. Whenever I get bored or want to fantasize about being outside of the therapy office, all I have to do is look at the picture. On another wall is a small painting of an isolated beach and the ocean in Hawaii. This painting is supposed to be calming. On a small wall near the window of the office I have my psychology license and two small lithographs of Stein cartoons. Both of these cartoons are actually used in many of my therapy sessions. The first one shows a rat-person lying on the couch. The caption below says: "Yolanda conquered her fear of mice by living for years with a dirty rat." A perfect example of exposure therapy! The second cartoon has a picture of a gift with a bow in the middle of the picture. Above the picture it says: "What happens when you live too much in the past or in the future?" Below the picture it states: "You miss out on the present." This is a great picture that helps people in cognitive therapy to change their thinking.

In my other office I have a number of nature photographs that I took. A picture of a waterfall, another of a sunset, one of flowers and one of trees covered with snow. Again, I think most of these pictures are calming. It also occasionally leads to the question: "Did you take these pictures?" I do think it is therapeutic for most patients to know that I have interests other than psychology.

I have two small things in my office that were given to me by patients. I have a framed five-by-seven inch picture of a sunset that a patient took and I have a six-inch high doll that has a little card attached. The doll is the "God of Anxiety." I figured it couldn't do me any harm to have this god in my office.

May 6

I had not heard from my patient who finished his virtual reality treatment for fear of flying a few weeks ago. He was scheduled to take a flight last week and I thought he would call me after the flight. I decided to call him today. He was a very happy man! He had successfully flown for the first time in years. He reported begin anxious but being able to utilize the techniques he was taught. The plane seemed very familiar to him after going through the VR sessions. I smiled to myself and put his success in my scorecard.

After finishing one session today a patient asked me if I would litigate her parking. I was a bit puzzled by this request. After initially thinking that I had to refer her to an attorney, I realized that she meant validate.

I have made the mistake of occasionally referring patients to service providers that I use and like. For example, I think my dentist is great. A number of years ago a patient was having dental problems and asked me if I knew a good dentist. I thought that it would be helping the dentist's practice and helping my own patient to tell him the name of my dentist. It turns out the patient was a pain in the ass in the dentist's office and argued with all of his staff. He then returned to my therapy sessions and complained about the experience he had. Confession number 119: Anytime a patient now asks, "Do you know a good _____?" I lie and say I really don't.

Another patient today wanted information about my penis. He asked if I knew what the end of my penis looked like. After answering him that I did know what it looked like, he informed me that the end of my penis was the same as his friend. His friend was a "dick head." I wonder if he could have just told me that without inquiring about my knowledge of my own penis.

I am thinking about adding another question to my list of all-time favorite questions. A patient asked me today; "Can I be honest?" I answered that honesty would be very helpful to the therapeutic relationship. I wanted to say that if the honesty had anything to do with criticizing your therapist that I would prefer that you lie.

May 8

I had to do an evaluation today with a patient who wanted to enter the UCLA OCD Program. I have probably done more than 500 of these evaluations. At this point in my career, I think I have a very good understanding of the diagnosis of OCD. After completing the evaluation I concluded that this patient's main problem was not OCD. She apparently did not like that conclusion and started arguing with me. "My current therapist says I have OCD! I also read a book about OCD and I think I have OCD." Who am I to argue with this reasoning? Unfortunately, one of my personality traits is a need to be right. So I discuss the issue with the patient. However, I cannot convince her that I am correct.

It is understandable that non-mental health professionals believe that any behavior or any thought that is repetitive is OCD. "Hey Joe, you always order the same drink every time we go to dinner. Do you have OCD?" "I just can't stop thinking about that beautiful woman in my office. I must be obsessed with her." "I can't stop eating. I must have OCD." However, each year I evaluate five to ten people who have been misdiagnosed by their therapist or psychiatrist. The therapist believes the patient has OCD and refers the patient to me.

As bad as the previous mistake is, it is far more devastating for a patient with a disorder like OCD to see a therapist for years and never be treated for the OCD. Some patients become very angry at their therapists when they find out they have OCD and have never been treated for it. In many cases it is probably malpractice on the part of their therapist. I had one patient who was in psychoanalytic treatment for twenty years and was never told that he had OCD and that there were effective treatments available for his problem. Unfortunately for the analyst, this patient was an attorney. They settled out of court.

Confession number 120: When I hear stories of incompetent therapists my first reaction is to scream, "Sue the bastard." I have learned to resist this temptation because of the fact that the patients may not have told me everything. In fact, there are times I believe that patients have blatantly lied to me. I assume these were not the patients who asked me, "Can I be honest with you?"

May 9

I have a new patient today who had made a very serious suicide attempt about a month ago and had just been discharged from an inpatient psychiatric unit. He actually seems like a nice fellow and I probably could help him overcome some of his depression. Unfortunately, he is from Iowa and has to return there in about four weeks. That means I have four weeks to teach him everything I know. Confession number 121: As much as I believe that you can change the way you feel by changing your thoughts, there is a big part of me that believes some situations are innately depressing. In this case I really can't figure out how to make Iowa seem appealing.

One of my patients today told me that she looked at me more as a mentor than a therapist. I guess that is okay with me as long as the going rate for mentors is comparable to psychologists. This patient actually wanted me to participate in a potential business deal she was putting together. I was very ethical and told her that doing that would be considered a dual relationship and that I could not participate. Unfortunately for me the deal sounded very good. I thought about telling her to call me back in a few years after I had retired.

My waiting list is growing. I have seven patients currently waiting for an appointment. I tend to feel a little guilty when this happens because I usually estimate the amount of waiting time the way restaurants do when you are waiting for a table. I underestimate the time. "Dr. Tarlow, I know we told you it would be twenty minutes about thirty minutes ago but there should be something coming up in about five minutes." This tends to keep you at the restaurant since it would be silly to leave now and try to find another restaurant. Most of these patients believe that I will see them in the next two weeks. That certainly would be possible if I decided to work on Saturdays.

May 12

Every now and then I try to use some clever analogies to bring home certain principles to my patients. For example, I tend to refer to obsessive thoughts as similar to junk mail. You don't have to open it and you can just throw it away. But, no matter how many times you throw away the junk mail you can't prevent it from coming back the next day. Obsessive thoughts are junk thoughts. You don't have to pay attention to them. However, that doesn't mean they won't come back the next day.

Another metaphor I use concerning the ability to be able to stop thoughts is the use of a Chinese finger trap where you place your fingers inside the ends of a cardboard tube. The harder you try to pull your fingers out the more "stuck" they become. In order to remove your fingers you have to relax them. This is similar to patients trying too hard to make a thought go away. The harder they try, the more persistent the thought.

I decided to use this metaphor in working with one of my patients today. I told her about the principle and then pulled the trick out of my drawer. After watching me pull my fingers out she asked if she could try. After a few minutes it was clear her fingers were stuck and she was not able to get them out. After I helped her remove her fingers she asked me if she could try it again in a few weeks. It seems like she missed the point of the exercise.

One of the strategies I use for patients who are having difficulty progressing in their therapy is to get them to talk to former patients who have been very successful in overcoming a similar problem. There are times this sort of motivation has worked very well. Today I had a very unusual request from one of my patients. She wanted to talk to a patient who had not been successful. I think she wanted to use the conversation to help her rationalize a decision to quit therapy. Confession number 122: There is no way that I am going to allow a patient who did not improve to talk to one of my current patients. I can imagine the following conversation in my calling up my old patient: "Hello, Mr. Failure. This is Dr. Tarlow. Remember me? I am the psychologist you spent $5,000 on and you didn't get any better. How would you like to do me a favor? I have a new patient who would like to talk to you about your experiences in therapy. You wouldn't mind? Is there any way you can convince him that it was entirely your fault that you didn't get better? No, you can't? Well thanks for listening to me. I'll try to never call you again to remind you of your failure." I tell my current patient that I don't think this approach would be very helpful and, thankfully she drops the request.

May 13

One of my patients today took about five minutes to tell me everything that was wrong in her life. It was quite a string of events ranging from her boyfriend leaving her, to developing cancer, to losing her job. Confession number 123: There are days when I hear these sad stories and my thoughts go back to the TV show *Queen for a Day* that I saw as a child. For those of you too young to remember the show, I will try to describe what took place. There were several contestants who would present their sad stories of all the bad things that had happened to them in their life. They were actually competing to see who had the saddest story. Stories such as my husband left me, my oldest son was arrested, they cut off my welfare payments, they turned off our heat, there were ten of us living in a one bedroom apartment, we got kicked out of the apartment because we couldn't pay the rent, we had to live on the street, and my youngest son got towed away because we were living in a no parking zone. The contestants would then be asked what they wanted if they were chosen queen for the day. Typically, they would request something that would have very little impact on their lives. "Well, if I were queen for the day I would want to take my entire family on a Caribbean cruise." There are days I listen to patient's sad stories and think this is the winner. This person is queen for the day.

Coincidently, today I received a brochure in the mail for a continuing education seminar titled "First Aid for Burnout and Compassion Fatigue." The brochure asks: "Are you afraid you are getting sick and tired of caring?" Maybe I have "compassion fatigue." Maybe I have heard so many sad stories that all of my empathy is drained. I picture going in for my next physical. "Dr. Tarlow, I am sorry to inform you that the results of our tests indicate that you have compassion fatigue. Your system is very low on empathy. Have you been doing anything that may have drained your empathy? You say you have been a psychologist for more than thirty years. We would recommend that you stick to utilizing only behavior therapy techniques. Please try to avoid the phrase "how are you feeling" when talking to your patients. If you follow these recommendations there is a good chance you will at least have enough empathy to use at home."

May 15

When I started practicing psychology, I did a great deal of psychological testing. Through the years I have done less and less. I recently received a request from a psychiatrist to do a complete evaluation, including psychological testing, on one of his patients. The evaluation is scheduled for today and includes an interview with the patient and the administration of several psychological tests. The test that I have the most experience with is the Minnesota Multiphasic Personality Inventory (MMPI). This test is a 566 item true-false exam that has been used for a long time to help determine diagnoses and treatment for psychiatric patients. I worked for eight years on the adult inpatient wards at the UCLA Neuropsychiatric Institute and administered approximately 2,000 MMPIs.

Many of the questions on the test are ones that you would expect, similar to "I feel sad a great deal of the time. True or False?" I have tried very hard in writing this book to not steal anyone's jokes. However, I can no longer resist. A number of years ago someone wrote a takeoff of the MMPI and called it the NNPI (No Nonsense Personality Inventory). Various versions of the test have been circulated among psychologists. I would like to share with you several of my favorite true-false questions from the test. (1) When I was younger, I used to tease vegetables. (2) I think beavers work too hard. (3) Recently I have been getting shorter. (4) I think I would like the work of a robot. (5) It makes me angry to have people bury me. (6) My tongue has been depressed. (7) It is hard for me to say the right thing when I am in a room full of mice. (8) My dog is someone else's best friend. (8) No napkin is sanitary enough for me. (9) I try to steal other people's thoughts and ideas when they are not looking. (10) I often use the word "feh." And, finally, (11) I never seem to finish whatever I

Another popular psychological test is the Rorschach inkblot test. This is the test where you look at an ink blot and tell the psychologist what you think you see. Since the test was developed it has been controversial. Many psychologists believe that it is not a scientifically valid test and therefore should not be used. Being an ethical psychologist it would be wrong for me to reveal what you should say when presented with an ink blot. However, Ooze Magazine, referring to the first inkblot revealed that "many disturbed people misidentify this blot as a misshapen hotdog, wounded mastodon or tax collector with a large Armani briefcase about to rape an ibex." Confession number 124: Personally, I have never received this response to a Rorschach card.

I complete the evaluation in about four hours. I decide not to use the Rorschach test. It will probably take another two hours to score the tests, write up the report and give feedback to the patient and the psychiatrist.

May 16

One of the wonderful things about being a psychologist is the variety of activities that can be included in your weekly schedule. Today I will be giving a guest lecture at a graduate class. I enjoy lecturing.

Unlike therapy sessions, I get to talk most of the time and people listen to me. My lecture today is on OCD. As part of my lecture I use a number of Gary Larson's Far Side cartoons to demonstrate examples of OCD. I have come to the conclusion that for Mr. Larson to create these cartoons, he either has OCD or knows someone who does. I have become a better lecturer over the many years I have taught. One of the nice things about lecturing about a topic you know so well is the ability to give the entire lecture without notes. The lecture goes very well and I get a great deal of positive feedback from the class. Driving home I start to think to myself that maybe I should do more teaching. Then the reality hits me that I would make about one-tenth the amount of money per hour if I decided to teach.

I return to my office to see a few patients in the afternoon. One of the patients informs me that he has just been told by his doctor that his eyesight has deteriorated to the point that he will never be able to read or drive a car. My empathy being replenished, I truly felt bad for him. We spend the entire session talking about how he can learn to cope with this problem and what pleasures he can still get out of life. There are times when my job is not to make people feel good, but to get them to feel less bad. The easiest way this can be done is with cognitive therapy techniques. One principle of cognitive therapy is that it is not the situation that makes you feel bad, but it is your interpretation, or thoughts, about the situation. If I can get a patient to see that their thoughts are distorted, I can help them to substitute more realistic thoughts. This particular patient responds very well to these techniques.

My last patient of the day has a major problem with cognitive therapy. He does not believe that thoughts can cause feelings. He tells me, "You just feel bad; there are no thoughts." After arguing with me for about fifteen minutes I realize that I cannot convince him of the validity of cognitive therapy. Confession number 125: I felt like I was arguing with my father. My father was a very stubborn, opinionated man. If a wall was white and he thought it was black there was no objective evidence in the world that could change his mind. I truly think that this patient needs to be referred to a therapist who is better able to tolerate irrationality. Unfortunately, I don't know any therapists who could tolerate this patient. Maybe I need to go online and do a search. I try the Google search engine and put in the words "irrational therapists." Alas, there are no hits. I decide to stop using cognitive therapy with this patient and stick to just trying to change his behavior.

May 19

Two of my patients today decided to bring food and they casually snacked during the session. I have had patients come into sessions and tell me that they didn't have time for lunch and do I mind if they eat during the session. This generally is not a problem unless I haven't eaten all day and I start to salivate. There is also the problem of what my office will smell like the following session. I am not sure that the smell of a sausage pizza enhances the therapeutic experience. There are some patients who are so busy eating that they have difficulty talking during the session. Confession number 126: There are times I want to take dishes and silverware out of my desk and start eating my own dinner when patients start to eat during the session.

Many more patients like to have something to drink during the session. Since this is LA the ubiquitous bottle of water often accompanies many patients. Some patients bring in their sixty-four-ounce cup of soda from the nearby 7-11. I usually just smile when I see this, knowing that I will usually get a five-minute break during the session so that the patient can use the restroom.

One of my patients today asked me the best question any patient has ever asked me. This was the second session for this patient for treatment of his OCD. He told me he was fully committed to the treatment but what he wanted to know was, "What was my commitment?" I thought for a moment and then told him that I was committed to seeing him at his scheduled time each week for forty-five minutes, unless I was on vacation. I was committed to making sure he received the best treatment available for his OCD. Between sessions I was committed to being available to answer any questions he may have about the treatment over the phone. I was committed to stay current on all the new research on the behavioral treatment of OCD. I was committed to treating him until he no longer required therapy. I felt my answer was good and so did the patient. Why did it take more than thirty years for a patient to ask me this question? I think that at times that the consumer of mental health services just assumes the therapist is committed to these things.

May 20

Sometimes patients decide to bring other people into their session. It is not unusual for a married patient to arrive at a session with his or her spouse. Many times having the spouse sit in on the session can be quite useful. Many parents often accompany their adult children to sessions. Sometimes they believe that their children will not tell me everything and that the parents can provide helpful information. I have only had one patient actually bring a friend into a therapy session. I think she was attempting to get her friend into therapy and wanted her to see me "in action."

None of these "therapy visitors" actually bother me very much. However, there are certain visitors that can be problematic. Today, I had a patient bring her baby to the session. Patients generally do this when they realize they do not have a baby sitter and they would have to pay for the session anyway because they didn't cancel with twenty-four-hour notice. Many parents bring their young children to sessions. If they are old enough the child can sit in the waiting room and play. If the patient has a very young child she often wants to take him into the session. In the past this has led to two problems. Have you ever tried to have a conversation while a child is crying loudly in the same room? Trying to do therapy with a screaming child is even more difficult. However, this is not the most difficult problem. Today was the second time in my years of practice that a mother decided to breast-feed during the session. I personally have no objection to women breast-feeding in public. The conflict I have is that in order to be a good therapist I need to make good eye contact with the patient. If a woman was breast-feeding in a restaurant I could take a quick look and then look away. In a therapy session I am looking constantly at the patient. Confession number 127: I find my eye contact is off by about a foot. Let's just say that the breast-feeding was not done subtly. I imagine an analyst would have a field day with this patient's behavior.

The other highly disturbing visitor during a therapy session is a dog. At first I thought that would be beneficial. We could spend five or ten minutes discussing dogs, thus shortening any therapy work for me. Several patients have brought their "well-trained" dogs to sessions. My eye contact with the patient is also disturbed during these sessions when the dog starts to walk around the office and I start to think that the dog is looking for a place to urinate. I must admit that no dog has ever urinated in my office. If it did happen I would have to invite more patients to eat their sausage pizzas during sessions in order to mask the smell.

May 22

At 4 p.m. today I see MW who informs me he is finally willing to quit doing his compulsive behaviors, on one condition. He is going to call a radio show hosted by a psychic rabbi. If the rabbi can identify his problem from his name and birth date he will be convinced that he will never have to do another compulsion. In ten years of therapy I have not been able to convince this patient to give up his compulsions so I am actually rooting for the psychic rabbi. I wonder what sort of training a psychic rabbi receives. Do you start with fortune cookies and move up to more difficult predictions?

There are actually a few things I have in common with the psychic rabbi. We both have professions that begin with psych. We both try to figure out what the patient's problem is. We both are Jewish. I wonder if new patients are ever confused. Maybe they thought they were going to see a psychic and ended up in a psychologist's office by mistake. Confession number 128: I am somewhat afraid to compete with the psychic rabbi. What if he is correct? As an ethical psychologist I would now have to tell all my patients that there is another type of treatment that may help them. I know his fees are a lot lower than mine. If he becomes really popular I wonder if he will write a book titled *Confessions of a Psychic Rabbi*. People will forget about me. Years from now people will read about ancient times when people went to therapists to talk about their problems, before the advent of the Psychic Rabbi Network. I don't know if I will sleep well tonight.

Sticking to this religious theme, LO, another of my patients today tells me that he admits things to me that he does not admit to anyone else. He tells me that therapy is like "confessional time." What if I could make it more like a confession for some patients? Maybe they could enter the office and start each session with "forgive me doctor, for I have screwed up." Just like a real confessional I could absolve them of their "screw up" and they could start the week with a clean slate. My father always wanted me to be a rabbi. This is probably as close as I could get.

May 23

I received an e-mail from a potential patient today. She wanted to know if she could get a reduced fee because she used to be the patient of a somewhat famous therapist and could tell me many good stories. This is the first time anyone ever asked me to reduce their fee because they had good stories to tell me. I certainly have had patients request fee reductions because they believed their cases were more interesting than anyone else's. Confession number 129: I think I should incorporate the following new fee schedule for all prospective patients:

(1) Ordinary run of the mill phobia......... $220

(2) Unusual phobia 175

(3) Typical auditory hallucinations............. 240

(4) Hearing Babe Ruth talk to you............. 125

(5) Anxiety without interesting stories........ 220

(6) Anxiety with interesting stories............. 150

(7) Borderline personality disorder........... 2750

(8) A never before seen mental illness .....FREE

I am seeing a patient today who I have not seen in about seven years. Getting calls from ex-patients is often disturbing. They generally do not call to just say hello and tell you how well they are doing. They generally call to tell you that all of their symptoms have returned and they are now worse than when you first saw them. That is the case for FP. FP is a forty-five-year-old married man who I helped get over a rather bad bout of depression. He was a very compliant patient the first time I saw him. I truly believed he learned the cognitive behavioral techniques and did not need me anymore. I tell all my patients that my job is to put myself out of business, but that I would never have to worry about that because we live in L.A.

I first need to retrieve his old file from storage. Although it may not be absolutely necessary, I have saved every patient file since I began practice. I don't think this is hoarding. I have received calls from patients that I saw fifteen to twenty years ago. However, the file cabinets in storage continue to grow. I have approximately five four-drawer file cabinets reserved exclusively for patient records. In one ethical-legal class I took, the presenter urged psychologists to keep their records forever, even after the psychologist died. We were told to designate someone to keep the records after our death. I imagine writing the following in my will: "I leave all my patient records to my son Michael to save for his entire life and then pass on to someone else in his will. If Michael cannot satisfy this requirement I leave all my patient records to my dog Casey on the condition that he does not use them to paper train any of his offspring."

FP is actually a very likeable patient for someone so depressed. The session turns out to be a "tune up." I gently remind him to do all of the same things I told him to do seven years ago. I am hoping I will only have to see him for a few sessions to get him back on track.

May 26

It is Memorial Day and I have the day off. I had to cancel eight patients today. I have lost approximately $1,600 in income. I spend most of the day playing golf and playing poorly. Confession number 130: I try to apply some of the cognitive principles I teach people in therapy to my golf game to help prevent me from throwing my clubs into the lake. Some of the self-talk goes like this: "Jerry, you know that last shot only went fifty yards when you wanted it to go 250 yards. Everyone makes mistakes. You have hit some good shots today and if you practice more you can become more consistent. Besides, throwing your clubs in the lake would probably trigger your social anxiety.

Everyone would be looking at you. People would be laughing at you. Just remember the positive things about golf. You are burning off at least thirty calories an hour getting in and out of the golf cart. You are with friends who are even worse golfers than you. You are a better golfer than Tiger Woods is a therapist. Enjoy!"

May 27

I completed therapy today with LH, a thirty-five-year-old married female with moderate symptoms of OCD. I thought it might be interesting to review her weekly behavioral assignments.

Week one: Drive to work taking a different route each day. This assignment actually created very little anxiety for the patient, but she was late for work three times.

Week two: Walk on the grass and then wear the same shoes into your house. I do not ask people to do this assignment at the dog park.

Week three: Do not check the chair after getting up. She initially did this at my office. I did find two quarters on the chair.

Week four: Tell a white lie without ever telling the other person that you lied. I think she told me that she forgot her checkbook and would bring it next week.

Week five: Use a public restroom and sit on the toilet seat without putting down one of those papers. We negotiated this assignment to include only certain public restrooms. The bathrooms on Venice beach were excluded.

Week six: Leave the oven on and leave the house for the day. I think I forgot to tell her to take the cake out first.

Week seven: Throw out magazines that had been hoarded. I think she just dropped them off in my waiting room.

Week eight: Park your car in a different parking spot at work. I think she got in a little trouble with this one. I don't think I asked her to park in her boss's spot.

Week nine: Have a bad thought when you walk through the door. I had to emphasize to not say it out loud.

Week ten: Read a novel for thirty minutes each day and purposely miss some of the words. For some novels I have read recently it might be easy to miss most of the words.

Week eleven: Leave the bathroom sink dripping slightly and then leave the house. It is important to show the patient what I mean by slightly. I don't think my malpractice insurance includes flooded houses.

Week twelve: Purposely make spelling mistakes in sending out e-mails. I am sure nobody noticed these given some of the spelling I receive on my e-mails.

Week thirteen: Pick out the first drink on the 7-11 shelf and drink it. You are of course allowed to wash your hands if you are touched by one of the people standing in front of 7-11.

Week fourteen: Go to the AIDS clinic, sit in the waiting room and read the magazines. This patient actually got kicked out of the clinic for not having AIDS.

Week fifteen: Bump into someone and don't ask if they are all right. You are not allowed to do this assignment in New York City.

Confession number 131: In proposing some of these assignments to patients, I often have to behave like a used car salesman. "For your assignment this week, I would like you to move all of the objects on your desk to a different position on the desk. No, you won't do that? How about just moving the stapler to the other side of the desk." My goal is to ask for the moon and settle for a few stars.

May 29

I received a call today from a potential patient. I find it interesting how some new patients present themselves to me over the phone. After talking to this person for five minutes, I knew I didn't want to see her in therapy. Confession number 132: There are a number of things that you should never say to a potential therapist during the first phone contact if you really want to see that person. Do not say, "I used to see Dr. Previous and I am now thinking of suing him for malpractice." Do not say: "Are you available twenty-four hours a day if I need to talk to you? My previous therapist gave me his home phone number." Do not say, "Do you clean your office after each patient leaves?" Do not say, "I just have a few more questions for you," and proceed to ask fifteen more questions. Finally do not say, "I don't think I can afford your fee. Would you mind billing me?"

I had several interesting quotes today from different patients.

- "Forget I said anything." Not the right thing to say to your therapist.

- "I am not in a chatty mood. You are going to have to pull teeth." I never wanted to be a dentist.

- "You don't understand me yet." Give me another three years in therapy and I am sure I will understand you.

- "My wife gave me a core dump." I think this is a science fiction term. Maybe from star trek. Definitely not a nice present.

- "Being normal is so boring." Sometimes boring is good.

I also received a call today from someone who wanted me to observe her husband. I do evaluations and obviously I observe patients during the evaluation. However, I do not do "observations." I imagine bringing the patient into my office and saying, "Please have a seat here behind the one way mirror. I will be observing you for the entire session behind the glass."

May 30

I have two patients today with the exact same problem. They both have OCD and specifically are afraid to drive. They both fear that they have hit someone when they are driving and then have to go back to check if there is a dead body in the road. Unfortunately they have to check in a very compulsive manner. One patient drives around the block to the spot where he thought he hit the pedestrian. He may have to drive around the same block ten times before he is convinced that nothing happened. The other patient has to get out of her car and carefully check the area for a body. She looks under cars and on the sidewalks.

As usual I give them both exposure assignments. One patient has to drive over streets with potholes and not check to see if he hit anyone. This tends to be a much easier assignment for patients to carry out in cities with bad roads. The other patient must drive in the right lane on streets with heavy pedestrian traffic and not drive around the block. My favorite all time exposure assignment for patients with this problem was developed by a psychologist in Florida who works extensively with OCD driving problems. Apparently, he throws mannequins in front of the cars of these patients while they are driving. I have never used this technique, but for it to be effective you could not tell the patient whether it was a mannequin or a real person. Confession number 133: I know a number of people whose help I would like to have in doing these exposure assignments by volunteering to be thrown in front of these cars.

Many of these patients also check the newspapers the next day for news of a hit and run accident. I could also place a false ad in the LA Times asking for information about a hit and run accident in the same area the patient was driving.

In working with OCD patients it is often easy to tell if they are resisting doing their compulsions. Patients who are compulsive handwashers have hands that are the color of an apple. Patients who check will often look around their seat when they get up to leave. Patients with driving OCD are often late for their session. I sometimes try to look out my window to see if they are driving around the block repeatedly.

Both of my patients today report that they are doing very well and are making significant progress in controlling their OCD. I give them both very similar driving assignments for the coming week. I hope they don't run into each other.

CHAPTER 9
June

June 2

One of my patients today, AR, is an 18-year-old male. Near the end of the session he says that he would like my advice about an important issue. He wants to know if he should get a tattoo and have his ear pierced. My first reaction is that this is very poor judgment. No, I don't mean the actual act of getting the tattoo or piercing. I mean asking someone over the age of fifty if one should do it. Since I have never been in the navy, the NBA, in prison and I don't ride a Harley Davidson, it is unlikely that I would have a tattoo. I try to be as objective as possible, but it is nearly impossible. How can I forbid my own son not to get a tattoo or piercing and help this person make an objective decision?

Last week I had a patient come into a session with green hair. His hair color was impossible to ignore and it led to an interesting discussion of why he changed his hair color. He told me that his mother had given him permission since he was very young to do whatever he wanted with his hair. He could shave it all off, grow it very long, or color it any way he wanted. She told him it didn't matter because it would always grow back. He told me that he has always experimented with his hair and therefore never had the urge to get a tattoo or piercing. Confession number 134: I wanted to tell AR that I didn't like the idea of a tattoo or piercing, but has he considered dying his hair green?

June 3

In becoming a psychologist, I believe it is a prerequisite to learn about dream interpretation. Although no patient comes to me for help with their dreams, I am often asked about the meaning of dreams. Objects appearing in dreams have been thought to be symbolic. For example, snakes have been thought to be symbolic of sex. Today I had a patient who was very concerned about a dream she had about being abducted by aliens. Confession number 135: I am not sure what aliens symbolize in a dream, but I am very familiar with all of the X File episodes concerning alien abduction. In fact the patient had already found a web site that talked about alien abductions when people were sleeping. She wanted to know if I believed this wasn't a dream. I wanted to know why psychologists can't provide antipsychotic medication to people like this.

My basic philosophy about dreams is that they are a reflection of what you recently experienced in your waking life. That is why we don't let children watch very scary movies. We believe that they will then have "bad" dreams.

I have discovered yet another way psychologists are being driven into extinction. If you go on the internet and search for dream analysis, you can have someone interpret your dream for a small fee, $35 at one web site I checked. Just think of all the dreams you could have interpreted for the price of a single therapy session with a psychologist.

June 5

Today I am treating a patient for a fear of flying by going on a commercial flight with her. The patient has not flown for over fifteen years but was getting pressure from her husband to fly. I pick the patient up at her house to drive her to the airport. This is a technique that I learned several years ago after waiting for two hours for a patient to show up at the airport. The therapy starts as soon as she gets in the car. I have to help her to change some very distorted thoughts about today's flight. She believes that the pilot is probably drunk, the plane is not safe and that the plane will crash and she will never see her family again. We quickly bypass the machine that sells flight insurance and make our way to the gate. The patient wants to know how much I charge if the return flight is cancelled. This is a good question that no patient has ever asked me before. It could get very expensive if the entire round trip takes twenty hours instead of three.

As we get on the plane I ask her to sit in the window seat. This is another strategy I have learned from a past mistake. I once had a patient bolt out of his seat and off the plane before I could get out of my seat belt. If I sit on the aisle this can't happen. Most fear of flying patients are most afraid of the takeoff. This patient is no different. I try to get her to relax and try to teach her about the various noises she is hearing. I also try to distract her away from the evacuation instructions given by the flight attendant. Confession number 136: I want to tell her that if the plane crashes into Bakersfield the seat cushion flotation devices will not be that helpful.

It is a short flight, about forty-five minutes in the air. The patient becomes more relaxed as the flight continues. She even wants to look out the window. I don't tell her about my favorite old Twilight Zone episode in which William Shatner looks out the window on an airplane and sees a creature messing with the engine.

The plane lands and the patient is overjoyed. We wait about thirty minutes and return to L.A. on another flight. The patient is even more relaxed on this next flight and has no distorted thoughts. She lands in L.A. and is now an officially "cured" phobic. She can't wait to go on a flight to somewhere she actually wants to go.

June 6

Keeping with the theme of finding alternative and cheap therapy, I found an interesting device while looking for a birthday card at a novelty store. It is called "My Analyst." It looks just like a Magic 8 Ball but it apparently takes the place of your therapist. I tried it out in the store by asking it how I could cure my fear of snakes. I shook it and turned it over and "My Analyst" said, "Tell me more." Confession number 137: After spending thirty minutes in the store with My Analyst I was convinced that it was about as good as half of the therapists that I knew.

Many years ago a few psychologists attempted to program computers to be therapists. The patient would type in their question or statement and the computer would pick up key words and then ask the patient another question. For example, you could tell the computer that you were feeling depressed lately and the computer would respond, "You have not been feeling very happy lately?" I remember trying out the program for the first time and telling the computer that it couldn't help me because it was just a stupid machine. The computer responded, "You are angry at machines?" Needless to say I have never recommended these computer therapists to any of my patients. However, it may be an option for a future patient who I don't like and wouldn't even refer to one of my enemies.

One of my patients today asked me about the books I had written that were displayed in my bookcase. I think the presence of these books increase my status in the patient's eyes. She wanted to know if I was currently writing a book. I did not particularly want to tell her about this book. There are a select number of patients who know I am writing this book. I didn't want this patient to know that I have written about her several times. I think it is prudent to just wait for the call from her attorney after the book comes out.

June 9

Today I received two of the best phone messages I have ever received. A patient who completed therapy a few months ago left me a message saying I had "changed her life." This is generally the best message a psychologist can ever get. However, the second message was almost as good as the first. A patient I intensely disliked left a message that he would not be returning to therapy and that I can give away his appointment time. I was overjoyed! Confession number 138: If this patient called back five minutes later and said that he had changed his mind I would have told him, "I am sorry, but I have already filled the time." I suppose that one of my deepest conflicts is a horrible patient who also pays my full fee.

I saw Mr. Green Hair in therapy again today. He works as a waiter in a restaurant. He informed me today that since his hair has been green his tips have increased. Confession number 139: I wonder whether I could charge more if I colored my hair green. My hypothesis is that I would actually lose patients. They would probably think I was too flaky. However, letting my hair go gray would probably help in my profession. People generally think gray haired men are more distinguished.

One of my patients today had a touch of paranoia. She believed that people were looking at her and thinking she was crazy as she walked down the street. Since I was starting to get a little bored in the therapy session, I recommended that we go for a walk so she could point these people out to me. In a brief walk, we passed about ten people and the patient told me that only one was looking at her. I actually thought about three or four were looking at me. No amount of reasoning could convince her that people were not looking at her. I referred her to a psychiatrist for this symptom. There are definitely some symptoms best treated with medications.

June 10

When I get patients from the waiting room I often ask them how they are. It is just a cordial greeting. I asked one patient today and received an answer I had never previously received: "Rich." This patient had just reached an agreement in a lawsuit. It has always been interesting to me how few patients ask me how I am doing.

I did an evaluation today of a patient for the UCLA OCD Program. He had a type of OCD characterized by the need for symmetry and exactness. His major symptom was that the toilet paper had to be torn off straight across. If this didn't happen it made him very anxious. He would actually go around to different bathrooms checking that the paper was torn correctly. Luckily, this was his only major symptom of symmetry. I have had other patients with this problem whose entire life was ruled by their need to arrange things in a certain order or put things in a certain place. The most severe case of this I ever saw was a woman whose house was as close to perfect as any I have ever seen. Most of her day was spent straightening and arranging objects in the house so that they were perfect. She would know if I had moved a vase one inch. Her boxes in her pantry were lined up from shortest to tallest. Her fruit was neatly stacked in her refrigerator. All of the silverware in her drawers was neatly stacked. Her clothes were all perfectly organized in her drawers and her closet. Unfortunately, she would also organize her husband's and children's possessions in the same manner. When I describe this patient's symptoms to people the most common response I get is: "Can she come over to my house for a few hours each day?" Confession number 140: I often have the fantasy of sending her over to the house of one of my hoarders. By the time she was finished either the hoarder's house would be neatly arranged or the hoarder would have killed her.

June 12

I received a call today from an insurance company asking me if wanted to do an independent evaluation for them. What is an independent evaluation? Theoretically, it is defined as an evaluation by a mental health professional who does not work for the insurance company or the insured. Hey, I am free to come up with my own conclusions. That is if I don't care whether I get any more business from that insurance company. How many calls from the insurance company will I get in the future if I determine that the patient continues to be disabled and the insurance company needs to continue to pay her? If you ever need an expert opinion it probably can be obtained no matter how ridiculous the opinion. For example, "Dr. Expert, you stated in your report that you believe the patient probably was from Mars and was not suffering from delusions at the time of the incident." "Dr. Expert, you reported that this patient is not depressed, has never been depressed and has not even been sad for one minute of his life. Is that correct?"

Being in court as an expert witness is probably one of the most profitable things a psychologist can do. You usually get paid for a half-day or full day in advance of your testimony. The rates charged for testimony tend to be two or three times the normal hourly rate. I assume that since the psychologist is in court he believes he should charge as much as the attorneys.

The insurance company seemed very pleased that I would do the evaluation. They asked if I would be interested in other evaluations.

Confession number 141: I am prepared to name my next house after the insurance company.

My son finished his school year today. This is an important milestone for me since a few years ago I set my retirement date as my son's graduation from college. That means I have 1095 more days of work remaining. But who's counting?

June 13

Insurance companies continue to demonstrate to me their ill will. When patients are admitted to the UCLA OCD program their treatment often has to be preauthorized by the insurance company. This means that I have to call the insurance company and give them the clinical information that I obtained from interviewing the patient. This sounds like a relatively simple procedure. However, the first problem is getting to talk to a live person. After being transferred about five times and being placed on hold for ten minutes, I was finally connected to a live person. This person took all of the demographic information on the patient and then told me I would be transferred to a case manager. After another five minutes on hold I was put through. The case manager informed me that since the patient was to be admitted on Monday that I needed to call back either the day before or the day of admission. I then proceeded to have an argument with the case manager over what was the day before. My contention was that since I don't work on Saturday or Sunday and that the OCD program is not open on Saturday and Sunday, that Friday is actually the day before. This logic appeared alien to him and he refused to take my clinical information. My other major point is that the information that I would give him today cannot change by Monday since I will not be seeing the patient during the interim. After years of dealing with insurance companies I honestly believe they will do almost anything not to not pay a claim or provide services that are justified. I have submitted claims to insurance companies and not heard back from them for sixty days. I call the insurance company and they say they never received the claim. I tell them, "That's funny, it had a return address on the envelope and I never got it back." They tell me that I can resubmit the claim. Even if they then pay the claim, they have had ninety extra days to keep their money. I often get back claims I have submitted with notations that I have left out information. The majority of the time the information has not been left out and I return the claim to the company. This gives the company an extra thirty days to process the claim

I also received a check today from an insurance company. It was for one cent. Confession number 142: I plan on not cashing the check and showing it to patients when they ask me if I can bill their insurance company.

June 16

I had two new patients today and they probably represent the extremes of patient likeability. The first patient was a young woman with severe confidentiality issues. As soon as I gave her the patient registration forms to fill out she started asking me if all of the information was confidential. I gave her a straightforward answer, which apparently did not suffice. She then started to ask about specific legal situations where I would be forced to reveal the information. Confession number 143: I really, really wanted to tell her that my policy was to make all information told to me available to the local press and that I also publish it over the internet.

After surviving the confidentiality questions, I realized that this twenty-four-year-old woman probably had a lot higher IQ than I do. She started to use these very big words that I had never heard in the therapy session. I wrote down some of the words to look up later to make sure she wasn't just pulling my leg. She also had this tendency to argue with everything that I said, including her diagnosis. After a while I realized that she was having fun with these arguments and appeared to relish my difficulty in responding to some of her questions.

The second patient was a very likeable older woman who was having difficulty passing her CPA exam. After describing her experiences to me I started to believe that she really did not need psychotherapy. It briefly ran through my mind that I wouldn't even charge her for this session. There have been only a few patients in all my years of practice who I did not charge for the initial session. If I really don't want the person as a patient I might not charge for the first session. If I truly felt I could not help the patient, and there were financial hardships I might also not charge. By the end of the session she decided that she would like to come back to see me.

My final patient today was angry with God. Apparently God was responsible for all of her problems. I have a difficult time with this concept, but it was made even more disturbing by the fact that she had to yell and scream at God in the session today. Although I am not very religious, after about twenty minutes of this screaming I started to be concerned that if God became really pissed at this patient he may see that I was in the same room and assume that I was also angry at him. In case he reads this book, I want to ensure God that I am not angry with him.

June 17

One of my patients today asked me if I had thought about his problem during the week. He jokingly said, "I know you spend all week thinking about me." You may wonder how much a therapist actually does think about a patient's problem during the week. The answer is quite simple. Unless you have presented your therapist with some imminent crisis, by the time you have finished your session and walked out the door your therapist is now focused on the next patient. By the time your therapist has seen eight patients for the day, your case is now in long-term memory.

I had one of the most enjoyable therapy sessions I have ever had today. A patient began the session talking about the recently concluded NBA playoffs. Since I love to watch sports, this conversation made me think of what it must be like to be a radio show sports-talk host. I am getting paid to talk about basketball! After about fifteen minutes of this talk I was beginning to feel a little guilty so I tried to change the topic. The patient then told me how much she admired the two photographs on the wall that I had taken. There were pictures of a waterfall and a sunset in Hawaii. She felt the pictures were very soothing and wanted to know where they were taken. This led to a thirty-minute discussion of the relaxing qualities of Hawaii. Every time I tried to change the subject the patient asked more questions about Hawaii. Before I knew it the session was over. Confession number 144: By the end of the session I was ready to move to Maui. I had convinced the patient to take her next vacation there. I also went home to find out how difficult it would be to change my occupation to a sports talk show host.

June 19

I finally had a follow up session with the patient who consulted the psychic rabbi. I was not surprised to find that the consultation was not very helpful. He told my patient that at times he gets angry. He told him that he has had some conflicts with his parents. He told him that he saw relationship problems in his past. Confession number 145: I wanted to tell the patient that the psychic rabbi failed to tell him that the sun will rise tomorrow or that he will have to use the bathroom in the near future.

In graduate school we learned about the Barnum effect. The effect was named after P.T. Barnum's quote that there is a sucker born every minute. In the experiment, an introductory psychology class is given a psychological test and then a week later called into the professor's office to discuss the results. The students were read a paragraph similar to the psychic rabbi's thoughts for my patient. The students were then asked to evaluate how accurate the interpretations were for them. Almost everyone thought the interpretations were highly accurate and specific to them. The Barnum effect is the basis for all psychics, astrologers, palm readers and some therapists.

I told my patient that since I saw him last I too had developed psychic ability. I asked him if he wanted a demonstration. I proceeded to give him my best two psychic predictions ripped off from Comedy Central. I told him that his great, great, great grandmother was no longer with us. I then wrote the word "no" on a piece of paper and asked him if he knew the word that I had written down. He immediately said "no." I showed him the piece of paper, took my bows and concluded the session.

June 20

When I answer the phone in my office, patients generally hear one of the following two greetings: "Center for Anxiety Management" or "This is Dr. Tarlow. Can I help you?" When I started in private practice in 1978, I wanted to find a name for my practice that would attract business. Utilizing this name probably has backfired. When you are called the Center For Anxiety Management, you have difficulty explaining to patients that you treat depression, eating disorders, marital conflicts, or anything else that is not officially an anxiety disorder. Confession number 146: Thinking back on my choice of business names I think I would have been better served with something different. How about The Center For Miraculous Cures of Emotional Problems? Since I eventually hired a number of assistants I could have called it Therapists R Us.

I tried very hard to come up with a name that would also be a cool acronym. Everybody loves a name like MADD (Mothers' Against Drunk Driving). At the time I just wasn't clever enough to think of one that included anxiety in the title. I think the best catchwords would be CURED or HELP. For CURED I could be the Center for Uncanny Relief of Emotional Disorders. For HELP I could be Hope for Emotionally Limited People. If my center were named HELP I could answer the phone: "Hello, you have just reached HELP."

The reason I started to answer the phone with "This is Dr. Tarlow" is that callers would often ask to speak to Dr. Tarlow. However, there are actually two Dr. Tarlows who work in the Center and I often have to ask the patient which Dr. Tarlow do you want to speak to? This is very confusing to many new patients since many of them have not been given a first name. They have just been told to call Dr. Tarlow. Based on the referring person I often can determine who they want to speak with. I don't mind these new patients being confused. However, I do mind when I answer the phone, "This is Dr. Tarlow, can I help you?" and the person on the other end asks if this is Dr. Nan Tarlow. Since my teenage son now has a deeper voice than I do I might just have him answer my phones for his summer job.

June 23

I can deal well with patients who are angry with other people. I have difficulty dealing with patients who are angry with me. I finally reached my breaking point with one of my patients. FG started to yell at me during the session. After I asked her why she was unable to accomplish her weekly goals, she shouted at me, "Use your brain!" She then went on to tell me that life sucks and that everyone is a fucking prick. Through the years patients have become angry with me for numerous reasons. The following is a list of some of the reasons: (1) I did not cure their problem by the second session. (2) I did not return their page while I was in session with another patient. (3) I wouldn't reduce their fee. (4) I notified child protective services that they had been abusing their child. (5) I sent their account to collections. (6) I had them hospitalized involuntarily as a danger to themselves. And (7) I smiled or laughed inappropriately.

This final reason occurred several years ago. During a session with a depressed, angry patient, I smiled at a comment the patient made. She immediately thought that I was mocking her and told me that she could not tolerate it. For the remainder of my sessions with this patient I would practice having a bland facial expression prior to every session. There were times after the patient left the session that I would just break out in laughter. It was if all my smiling and laughter was bottled up for forty-five minutes and then came bursting out.

There are times I can tolerate a patient's anger at me. I can use that anger to help a patient look at the irrational thoughts that led to the anger and help the patient change those thoughts. Then there are the occasional times I get defensive and counter-attack. Confession number 147: Here is the counter attack I would use with FG if pushed to the limit: "Use my brain! At least I have one that works."

June 24

It's time for another update on some patients. LO returned from a one-month vacation and his OCD was the same as it always was. You might think that a nice relaxing vacation would do wonders for patients. Unfortunately, LO just left his OCD at home and picked it up when he returned.

CK no longer wants to work on his OCD. He is too depressed because he is unable to find work. I just pray he doesn't start thinking that it may be a good idea to change professions and become a therapist.

BD also does not want to work on her OCD. She is still very concerned about her daughter's financial situation. Let's see, if she cancelled all of her therapy appointments with twenty-four-hour notice she would easily be able to supplement her daughter's income.

FK is an OCD patient who is having difficulty understanding some of the behavioral assignments. His initial assignment was to leave the toaster plugged in all night.

EL continues to work on his hoarding. Today we are working on discarding catalogs that are sent to his house. I get to look through the catalogs and get paid for it!

TH wants to work on her fear of elevators. I tried some paradoxical therapy today with her. Another name for paradoxical therapy is reverse psychology. I told her that she really didn't want to get better and there was no sense in trying. Unfortunately, this technique backfired when she agreed that I was correct.

Confession number 148: Scorecard: I rated five of the six sessions as good or excellent work on my part. I wish my softball batting average was this good.

June 26

One of my patients today is a real success story. He is about thirty-five years old and just found out this week that he was accepted into medical school. He started taking pre-med classes about six years ago after becoming frustrated with the jobs he had since graduating college. He continued to work full time and take courses at night until he fulfilled the pre-med requirements. One of the enjoyable things about this patient is his sense of humor. He has a wonderful ability to laugh at everything, including his own problems. This attitude makes him the type of patient a therapist looks forward to seeing on his schedule.

In shrinking this patient today, he asked me if I had ever been in the city where he was going to attend medical school. I told him that I was there in 1967 and he said, "When you were five years old?" Confession number 149: I believe it is a rule of therapy that when your patient thinks you look younger than you are they should be given a discount on their fee.

I asked the patient if he intended to become a psychiatrist. He replied, "If I had to listen to people whine and complain all day long I would kill myself." Again, this patient earns more points. He can actually empathize with how his therapist sometimes feels.

I have one more session with this patient prior to his leaving for medical school. It will be hard to terminate with him. I will miss seeing his name on my schedule.

June 27

This morning is very different. I am one of three examiners for a psychologist who is trying to pass his diplomate exam. It is an exam that I took about six years ago. It is the second time I have been asked to be an examiner. The exam is completely oral and takes about three hours. The examiners are free to ask just about anything of the candidate. When I took the exam I actually enjoyed the process. It felt as though I was just having a good conversation with a few psychologists whose orientation was very similar to my own. They were also truly interested in whether I was competent in the areas of my practice. Even as an examiner I am able to learn new things from the other people in the room.

The candidate today was actually a psychologist who I knew about twenty years ago but have had little contact with since then. My first problem in the exam was that this psychologist was the spitting image of Kevin Costner. Confession number 150: When I asked him about any mistakes he had made professionally, I half expected him to tell me that he never should have made *Water World*.

The second problem I had with this candidate was that it was difficult to get him to answer a question directly. He had so much experience in administration that he had become more of a politician than a psychologist. I would ask what I thought was an interesting and specific question and he would start to answer the question and then wander all around the subject. By the end of the answer he could have been talking about Krispy Kreme doughnuts. I then would try to figure out how he got there but by the time I did he would be talking about something else.

The final problem I had with this candidate was that he knew very little about treatment with adults. I guess just because many people call me a "know it all" that I shouldn't assume that every psychologist is similar. I ended up passing him on the exam.

June 30

I had three cancellations today and that means more time to write this book. This is actually the fourth book I have written. The first book was titled *Using Psychology*. I was asked to co-write the book by one of my undergraduate professors at UCLA. He had written the first edition and wanted me to revise it. It was a book that was used in introductory psychology classes which is a rather large audience. I finished the revision in about three months and started to collect royalties within a year.

This experience led me to start my own book. I wanted to write a book for therapists and I wanted it to be useful. I wanted it to be a book that any behavior therapist could pick up and instantly find out how to assess and treat any problem ever treated with behavioral therapy. I wanted this book to define my career in psychology. This was truly a grandiose vision. I started the book while I was working full time at UCLA. Any time that I had a few extra hours I would go to the library to do research for the book. I hired students to help me find articles relevant to each chapter. Finally, after seven years of research I had completed the book. My publisher thought it would sell better as two volumes, so in 1989 the *Clinical Handbook of Behavior Therapy: Adult Psycholological Disorders* and the *Clinical Handbook of Behavior Therapy: Adult Medical Disorders* were published. I was very proud of the achievement. If only I had spent as much time picking a publisher as I did doing the research. In the following three years I made less money from these two books combined than the first book I revised. I also ended up having to hire an attorney to try to get the publisher, Brookline Books, to pay the royalties owed me. I saved one of the letters the president of Brookline Books, Milton Budoff, sent to my attorney, who happened to be female, during the course of the lawsuit. In reading the following excerpts from this letter please keep in mind that Dr. Budoff was not just the president of Brookline Books he was also a psychologist. "Your horseshit antics are finally provoking this response.... I am not interested in your testosterone-driven harassment.... I have a lawyer lined up and have briefed him. His firm has already beaten your guys—you are one of them, right—Miss Penis Envy? ... I do get a pleasant buzz from calling you what you are. My unhappiness is not having yet poked you in the mouth, a pleasure denied me by the distance. ... So stop the horseshit. Is that masculine street language enough for your testosterone wish/needs? Very Sincerely, Brookline Books Inc. By: Milton Budoff President"

Confession number 151: Yes, even psychologists can be assholes.

CHAPTER 10
July

July 1

In most large office buildings the public bathrooms are often locked. The office building that houses my West L.A. practice is no exception. In order to get into the public restrooms the patients need to borrow the keys that are hanging in the waiting room. One of my patients today informed me that the key to the women's restroom was missing. It is not the first time this has happened. In fact, through the five years I have been in my current office, the key has disappeared about twenty times. It is important to understand that the key is attached to a plaque approximately eight by twelve inches in size and labeled either men's or women's. I have a great deal of difficulty picturing people trying to put this key and plaque into their pocket or purse. I have a great deal more difficulty trying to picture them finding this key when they returned home and wondering what to do with it. "Oh, that must be a key to Dr. Tarlow's restroom. I'll just throw it out."

Since these keys often disappear and never reappear, I must assume that people are stealing the keys. In a continuing effort to thwart these key thieves, we generally attach larger and larger objects to the key. Confession number 152: I have the idea of attaching a full size car tire to the key. Patients could just roll the tire to the bathroom and back. Better yet, maybe I could employ the principles of behavior therapy to get people to return the key. Aversive conditioning works in keeping dogs within a confined area. Every time the dog leaves the area he is shocked. I could invent an attachment that automatically sends the patient a shock upon entering the elevator.

I received a call from the mother of a potential new patient today. After informing her of the type of therapy I do and the locations of my offices, she asked me where I live. I felt this was a rather intrusive question since I had absolutely no therapeutic relationship with this person. I declined to answer her question, but I thought afterwards that I should have just said "Fresno."

July 3

Today I had an extremely interesting contrast between two patients. One patient was successfully completing his treatment. He was very happy with the changes he had made in eliminating his panic attacks and reducing his fears in general. He made sure to praise me profusely for the help I had given him. The very next patient was extremely angry with me for what she felt were my failures as a therapist. She told me that I didn't appear to be committed to the therapy process, that I neglected to help her with two very crucial problems and that I was responsible for her inability to submit her insurance claims to her insurance company.

I have learned to listen very intently to all of a patient's complaints before responding. I must admit that in some cases it takes a great deal of will power not to interrupt the patient. I then have to decide how to respond. Given my personality, the response is typically to defend myself. Although the patient complained that I was not committed to the therapy process, she had only had ten sessions in the past year. She had cancelled approximately ten other appointments during the year. It is hard enough to work with people who only want to come in every other week. I was seeing this patient less than one time per month.

How do I work on a problem area that the patient has never discussed? "Dr. Tarlow, I am very upset that we have not dealt with my fear of eating broccoli during our sessions." "I am sorry, Ms. Thepoint, but you told me that your problem was that you had a fear of public speaking." Confession number 153: I probably should go back for those psychic training classes.

Finally, her asking me to refund the money she paid for a session two years ago because she was unable to submit the paperwork to the insurance company is one of the most creative and ludicrous requests that a patient has ever made. It is the ultimate example of the inability of a patient to take responsibility for her own life.

July 4

It is the start of another vacation. I will try not to think about psychology for the next 12 days. Just about every patient wanted to know where I was going. I felt comfortable telling most of them my location. For the others I just made up the silliest trips I could imagine. "I will be taking a road trip to Iowa and Kansas. I have never been there before."

July 14

I return from vacation and have the usual 30 phone calls to return and fifty pieces of mail to open. As always my first day back is booked solid with eight patient hours. At least three patients realized I was gone and asked me about my vacation. One of my patients today asked me for my opinion of hypnosis to discover what she was in a past life. I had previously put some thought, about ten minutes, into the subject, so I was able to offer her my educated opinion. It seems like most people find out that they had a very pleasant job or ordinary life in their past life. Imagine if you found out that in a past life you were a serial killer that had never been caught. If you believed that how would you live with the guilt? Even worse, what if you found out that in a previous life you were an attorney. I keep thinking I was probably a Jewish psychologist from Boston in a previous life.

I figure that past-life regression is a very profitable type of psychotherapy. After a patient finds out about their previous life, I am sure they would be interested in the one before that, then the one before that, then the one before that, etc. How does a past-life therapist estimate how long it will take to complete therapy? "Well, Mr. R. E.

Gression, it will take approximately ten sessions per life. And, I can offer you a discount once it gets to twenty or more lives."

Although I try to schedule most of my favorite patients for the day I return from vacation, there is inevitably a patient who reminds me why I should retire soon. My two p.m. patient decided to take on this role. She spent most of the session yelling at me and criticizing my inability to help her. After logic and reasoning seemed to fail, I asked her why she wanted to continue in therapy with such an incompetent therapist. She replied that it was her mother's idea. I finally told her that I would be happy to call her mother and convince her that she could no longer benefit from therapy sessions with me. Confession number 154: I always like to make recommendations upon the completion of therapy. I thought I would recommend to this patient's mother that she try one of the following options with her daughter: (1) a good exorcist, (2) a lobotomy, or (3) a French therapist who does not understand English.

Another patient today started to write me a check for the session, but had to write the check over after he realized he was paying me what he usually pays his gardener. I had the urge to ask him if that was more or less than my fee, but I resisted.

July 15
WARNING!!! DO NOT READ ABOUT THIS DAY PRIOR TO EATING.

I had a new referral today of a patient who has a sexual deviation and was told that I was an expert on covert conditioning. Covert conditioning is an interesting technique developed about forty years ago by the psychologist Joseph Cautella. It is an aversive conditioning technique that takes place in imagination. The goal of the technique is to pair the unwanted image (e.g. having sex with a child) with a truly unpleasant scene. One of the therapist's tasks is to help the patient create an unpleasant scene. One commonly used scene involves the patient vomiting all over himself, smelling the vomit, having the vomit go up his nose and back into his mouth. This scene is described in graphic detail. Dr. Cautella published a guide to help therapists create these scenes. The therapist asks the patient how much the patient is bothered by each scene. Some other examples of covert scenes include: imagining maggots crawling all over your food, seeing a dog on the side of the road with its guts hanging out, and seeing large rats crawling all over your body.

I always figured this list was incomplete after viewing the movie *Sleeper* with Woody Allen. The story takes place in the future and Allen's character is asked about a picture of Howard Cosell. He tells his examiner that, in his day, listening to Cosell was a means of torture. Confession number 155: I have developed a few additional scenes that could be used during the aversive conditioning: a videotape of a George Bush speech, eating a meal at Taco Bell, a picture of Rosie O'Donnell in a thong, and (my personal favorite) the sight of a teenager's room.

The technique has been expanded to include an aversive smell in conjunction with the scene. Some of the commonly used smells include: a rotten egg, a piece of meat left in the sun for a few days, and dog feces. The only problem with using these smells in a session is that your office stinks for about the next three days.

July 17

I treated a severely depressed patient today. One of the techniques that I used with this patient is called Pleasant Events Scheduling. It is a rather simple technique based on the theory that if people participate in pleasant activities they will reduce their depression. As the depression gets better they will want to participate in more and more pleasant activities. Peter Lewinsohn, the psychologist who created the technique, developed a list of 320 events that people rate for the degree of pleasantness and the frequency in which they engaged in the events. Examples of events include having a good talk, reading a novel, and watching television. A number of years ago one of my patients with a good sense of humor told me the list was incomplete and gave me her supplementary pleasant events schedule. Some of the events on her list included going naked, going to a sports event, going to a sports event naked, being with animals, kissing a sheep, having a meaningful relationship with a water buffalo, social drinking, antisocial drinking, and taking a philodendron to see a movie.

In utilizing this technique one of the therapist's tasks is to help the patient schedule the pleasant activities into their day. Many patients have difficulty in deciding when to do their pleasant activities. Therefore, it is my job to tell them that I think it would be a good idea to look at the moon and stars at night rather than at two p.m. Also, "maybe you can hold off on snow skiing for a few months."

Each week I attempt to add more pleasant activities into the patient's schedule. Confession number 156: When the patient is doing 137 pleasant activities each day and is still feeling depressed I tend to abandon the technique. It is at these times that I believe more in the concept of a "biological depression." I once asked a psychiatrist what would happen to a biologically depressed patient if he won the lottery. He told me that the patient would feel better for about a day.

July 18

I received a call today from a reporter with the L.A. Times. He wanted to do a story on psychosurgery for OCD. I know quite a bit about OCD but very little about psychosurgery. He still managed to interview me for about twenty minutes about the treatment of OCD. I very much enjoy being quoted in the newspaper. I even achieved a lifelong goal many years ago by getting my name in the sports section. Unfortunately, it was not for my athletic prowess. A reporter had called me to get my opinion of why John McEnroe had temper outburst on the court. One of the negative things about television and radio interviews is that they may last a long time but you are lucky if one or two lines are actually used. You also have no idea what line will be used.

Every now and then I call a patient and receive one of those annoying messages. "The party you called does not accept calls from blocked numbers. To reveal your number hang up and dial *82." This presents a small problem for me when calling from home or my cell phone. I certainly do not want the patient to have either of these numbers. I tend to leave some strange messages on my home answering machine and I might be embarrassed to have a patient hear one of them. I have had patients call me at home because they got my number from their caller ID. By the way, I think it is interesting that it is caller id and not caller ego or superego. My solution to this problem was to install a fax line in my home. If I call a patient from the fax line and she happens to call back on that number she will get a fax tone. I never answer the fax line. Confession number 157: I have the desire to change my outgoing message on my office answering machine to: "This is Dr. Tarlow. I am unable to answer the phone right now. Please leave your name and phone number after the tone and I will be happy to return your call as soon as possible. If you have call blocking on your phone I will return your call after you call the phone company to remove it."

July 21

There are times I get a feeling that a new patient is not going to work out well. I received a call a few weeks ago from a woman identifying herself as a doctor. Instead of leaving me a message on my answering machine, she decided to page me. It would seem to me that anyone who was a doctor would understand that she was already abusing the paging principles. Upon calling her back she immediately began to quiz me on my academic background, the type of therapy I do, and my experience. After practicing for more than thirty years I honestly don't think it matters whether I did my undergraduate work at Harvard or the University of Antarctica. After telling the patient that I had an office in Calabasas she wanted to know if I lived in Calabasas and exactly where I lived. It sounded like she would like to come over and visit some weekend. She wanted to be seen in Calabasas but I had no openings at that office. I told her I could see her in West L.A. and gave her a specific time and date. She told me she worked that day and would get back to me if she could make that time. She never called back to confirm and I therefore gave the time to another patient.

This morning the patient pages me again wanting to know directions to my office so that she can get to the two p.m. appointment. The only problem was that she didn't have a two p.m. appointment. I told her that it must have been a miscommunication. At that point she told me how valuable her time was and asked, "Don't you have a secretary who handles your appointments?'" I found myself becoming more and more enraged at her sense of entitlement. I finally told her that I refused to see her, but she refused to stop talking. At that point I did what every good passive-aggressive person would do: I hung up on her. Confession number 158: I felt great! I sacrificed a potential patient for the ability to stand up for myself. If only I could get some of my patients to do the same thing.

July 22

I am one step closer to accomplishing one of my new year's resolutions. UCLA Academic Personnel informed me today that my application for advancement from Associate Clinical Professor to Clinical Professor had been approved by the final committee and only needed to be signed by the dean. As with most things at UCLA, this step will take much longer than it should. I was told that it would take sixty days to get the dean's signature. That would put my official date of advancement somewhere in September of this year. Just for fun I decided to look at the date that I originally submitted my application for advancement. It was two-and-one-half years ago. Two-and-one-half years to decide! I now know why there are so few full professors in the Department of Psychiatry. Initially, I had to get ten letters of recommendation. Five of these letters had to be from people outside of UCLA. Confession number 159: It seems like everyone I know has some connection to UCLA. It is difficult to walk up to people on the street and ask for a letter of recommendation. I also do not think they would look very favorably on a letter from one of my ex-patients comparing me to Mother Teresa.

Part of the holdup was that no one in the Department of Psychiatry had time to request the letters from the ten people I chose. I was not allowed to contact the people I had listed as references to get them to mail a letter of reference to UCLA. UCLA informed me that if I did that, it would bias their evaluations. As it turns out, most of them sent me a copy of the letter they submitted on my behalf. You may want to know what the advantage of this promotion is. Is it a huge raise in salary? No! Is it a tenured position? No! Do I get a better parking space? No! Do I get tickets to UCLA sporting events? No! Do I get to tell everyone I know that I am a full professor at UCLA? Yes!

July 24

One of the nice things about many of the OCD patients I treat is that they have a very good sense of humor. Today one of my OCD patients brought in a cartoon he had created. It was labeled "the (O) CD ready car." The cartoon showed a picture of a car with the following features: self-locking, automatic turn-off lights, electronic counter (in multiples of three) and, of course, an anti-theft alarm. Naturally, the car was priced at $33,333. This is my kind of patient. He is able to laugh at his own disorder.

It has been a good week for telling patients jokes. Confession number 160: I have some very specific rules for telling and listening to jokes with patients. I tell Jewish jokes only to Jewish patients and male chauvinist jokes only to male chauvinist patients. I never attempt to tell a suicidal patient a joke. If, after giving a patient a therapeutic assignment, he asks, "Are you joking?" I always answer "Of course." And, I always laugh at a patient joke, even if it is not funny.

Everyone has his or her favorite psychologist joke. The following is mine: What do psychologists say to each other when they meet? You're fine, how am I?

July 25

I have the unpleasant task today of calling a patient who did not pay her bill for the services I provided in the UCLA OCD program. I left four messages for the patient's mother during the week and was finally able to reach her this morning. The mother informed me that she had paid my bill before her daughter entered the program and that the admissions department assured her that she would not be billed for any other services in the program. I told her mother that this sounded very strange and I would check into it for her. When I contacted the admissions office, I was assured that they never said that to the patient's mother and they knew that I did my own billing for the program. I asked the admission office to please call the patient's mother and inform her of what was said. I called the patient's mother about two hours later and asked if she received a call from the admissions office. She informed me that she did and they told her exactly what I told them to tell her. She also told me that she still had no intention of paying the bill. At this point I had to instantly decide on a strategy to use with this person. Here are my choices: (1) Continue to try to reason with her. Not a good choice since she apparently suffers from inability to listen disorder. (2) Take her to small claims court. Also a poor choice since she does not live in this country. (3) Send her to collections and attempt to ruin her credit rating. Or (4) do what every Jewish parent has done to his or her offspring since the beginning of time; induce guilt! I chose number 4. "Mrs. Deadbeat, I don't intend to take you to court for $600. If this is the way you pay me back for the services I provided your daughter, then so be it. I feel sorry for you and your daughter." Confession number 161: This strategy hardly ever works. Most likely because none of the people I try it on are Jewish. After trying it today I decided to just hang up on the patient's mother as she started to respond. About an hour later I received a call from her telling me that I appear to be in need of my own services. A novel approach, but how much do I charge myself? What happens if I don't want to leave the session on time? What if I don't pay my own bill? How can I tell when I am truly cured? I had a strong desire to call her back to let her know that I now understand how her daughter became so disturbed. I restrained myself. I guess that's similar to treating myself.

July 28

An OCD patient today brought in a book she was reading titled *The Thought Police.*

At first I thought the book was about OCD. Maybe there was a technique to help patients that I was missing. What if there really were thought police? Would they arrest people for having bad thoughts? Would there be a three strikes law where there would be some kind of gigantic punishment for having three episodes? Could the psychologist threaten a patient that if they continued to obsess, the thought police would be called? "Yes, is this the thought police? This is Dr. I.M. Incompetent. I have a patient in my office who is having bad thoughts. Can you come get him right away?" There would definitely have to be more severe penalties for certain thoughts. If you have an obsession about harming a child it has to have a greater punishment than an obsession about your hands being contaminated. Confession number 162: Psychologists also have bad thoughts. And yes, many of them are about our patients.

BP told me that his wife was out of town today. He said that she had left on her broom. I was hoping that his wife did not have a fear of flying on brooms because I had never treated that problem before. I also was not sure if brooms come with any frequent flier mileage.

MG is another OCD patient. One of her fears involves feeling that bad things will happen to her if she kills ants, spiders or any bugs. In order to help her overcome this obsession I needed to ask her to purposely kill some ants this week. She told me that she thought this would be difficult for her to do. I asked her what she would do if ants were all over the inside of her house and all over the food in her house. She informed me that she would then just hire an exterminator. I get it, a hit man! You hire a hit man to take care of all your problems, and then you don't have to feel bad. I tried my hardest to convince her to kill the ants, but in the end she refused. I couldn't convince her that she wouldn't go to hell for using Raid.

July 29

One of my patients today wants to talk about her lack of ability to be assertive with her father. Lack of assertiveness is a problem I have helped patients with since I began seeing patients in graduate school. Many of the techniques I employ are from the book *When I Say No I Feel Guilty* written by Manuel Smith. I truly think it is one of the best self-help books ever written. I also believe that most people, even the three people in the world who aren't in therapy, can benefit from utilizing the techniques in the book. The title of the book fits most of my patients in need of the techniques.

One of the techniques in the book is called "broken record." It is designed to help people get their needs met by being persistent. The technique basically consists of repeating your request, in the same words, numerous times until the other person finally succumbs. One of the best questions a patient ever asked me was: "What if the person you are talking to has learned the same technique?"

Another important technique to learn is how to deal with criticism. When I ran an assertiveness training group at UCLA I would ask the group to criticize my appearance so that I could show them how to assertively respond to the criticism. Confession number 163: I had to stop doing this in the group because after a round of Let's Criticize the Therapist I always had to go home and throw out all of the clothes I was wearing during the session.

It is sometimes hard to imagine how some problems affect patients the way they do. When I taught graduate students how to do assertiveness training, I would always have the graduate students do a few simple exercises in order to experience what an unassertive patient feels. I had them go into a restaurant, sit at the counter and order a glass of water. Or, I had them go to a Mercedes Benz dealer and ask to test drive the most expensive car in the lot.

July 31

It has been a week of many patients terminating therapy. On Monday I received a call from a patient I had seen nine times informing me that he would not be returning to therapy. In his message he told me that he thought the therapy was not working. He said I could call him back to talk about it, but his mind was made up. I truly believe that this person suffers from very bad OCD and will get worse if not treated by a good behavior therapist. Confession number 164: I never let patients hear this pessimism if they have already decided to terminate therapy. I returned his call and just told him that I hoped he got some help for his problem.

A second patient terminated treatment on Monday because he was too busy to do the OCD therapy assignments. A number of extremely stressful events occurred in his life over the past month and he found that he had no time to complete his weekly assignments. Chances are he will be back in therapy soon.

A third patient terminated therapy because she was actually done with treatment. She was truly a superstar patient. She "bought" the therapy philosophy, did all the therapy assignments, and started to feel much better. It took only three months of therapy. Her insurance company should throw me a celebration dinner.

And then, finally, RA terminated therapy because she was moving to another state. I had seen RA on and off for about eleven years. She was one of my favorite patients. She was able to laugh at her own problems and her own behaviors. But she was also able to see that she could make changes in her behaviors and her thoughts that would greatly influence her moods. Ending any eleven-year relationship is difficult. Throughout the last session I kept thinking that I would like to give her a hug when she leaves. Then I realized that during the course of treatment she had sued about forty different people and I never got out of my chair.

CHAPTER 11
August

August 1

Confession number 165: There are many times in the course of therapy that I have to help patients to become better liars. Here are some of the most common questions that patient's ask and my psychopathic responses.

"Dr. Tarlow, how do I tell my boss that I am coming for weekly therapy session?'

"Well, Mrs. D.Ceit, you just need to tell him that you have a Dr. appointment."

"Dr. Tarlow, how do I fill out the questions on my job application where they want to know what I have been doing for the past seven years while I have been depressed?"

Well, Mr. I.M. Alier, you just tell them about the college courses and extensive traveling you have done for the past seven years."

"Dr. Tarlow, I can't tell my wife I am in therapy. She doesn't approve of it."

"Well, Mr. Wimp, just tell her that you are spending $200 a week for a call girl."

"Dr. Tarlow, I can't tell my husband I am having an affair. What do I tell him when he asks where I have been every night this past week?"

"Since you are in need of extensive therapy Mrs. Slut, why don't you just tell him you have been to see your therapist?"

I have become a better liar myself. There are definitely things patients do not want to hear, even if they are true. One strategy is to phrase these things in such a way that the patient does not realize he or she has just been criticized. Another possibility is to just tell them an outright lie. "Dr. Tarlow, how long will this therapy take?"

"Well, Mrs. Nuts, if you work hard and do all of the therapeutic assignments and continue to take the medications that the psychiatrist prescribed, then I think it should take just a few months." Of course the truth is the following: "Mrs. Nuts, if I see you every day for the next ten years, and you take the forty-two prescriptions the psychiatrist has given you then I believe you should be able to get out of bed and eat meals by then. However, forget about ever having a friend."

August 4

I wake up in the morning to find myself quoted, or should I say misquoted, in the L.A. Times. As I suspected, my twenty minutes of interview time yielded about two lines of press. The first thing they got wrong was my title. After painstakingly making sure the reporter knew I was Director of Psychological Services at the UCLA OCD Program, in the article the reporter stated that I was Director of Psychiatric Services. Why is it that people still don't know the difference between psychologists and psychiatrists? My favorite response to that question when asked by someone other than a patient, is $40,000 a year. I now have to go back to UCLA tomorrow and tell them that I did not tell the reporter I was Director of Psychiatric Services.

The second major problem with the article was that it appeared that I was also talking about using "thought-blocking" therapy to treat OCD. First of all, there is no such technique as "thought-blocking." Also, it is well known that thought suppression, or just trying to prevent yourself from having certain thoughts, really does not help

OCD patients. When one of my patients today asked me about why I had said these things in the article I told him I hadn't and that I would have been better off if I had some OCD and insisted that I check what the reporter was going to write before it was published.

Even with the mistakes in the article, the publicity is good for business. I am swamped with calls for evaluations and therapy. One potential patient was extremely interested in my fees. She questioned me for approximately five minutes about my fees and wanted to know if there was any way I could reduce my fee. At the end of the conversation she told me that she had a few other therapists she was going to call and find out about their fees. Clearly this person was therapist shopping. Confession number 166: I had an overwhelming urge to shout: "You get what you pay for!" prior to hanging up with this patient. The longer I practice psychology the more I believe this cliché. However, there are exceptions to this principle. I recently learned of a marriage and family therapist in L.A. who charges $1167 for a forty-five minute session. This is the highest fee I have ever heard of for a therapist or psychiatrist. Imagine the ego it must take to charge three to four times the fee that experienced, well-respected therapists are charging.

August 5

Several patients over the past two weeks have asked me questions regarding their eating problems. I used to have a great deal of interest in eating disorders. When I left full-time employment at UCLA in 1986 I was involved in starting two different eating disorder programs. The 1980's could be called the decade of the eating disorders. It seemed like everyone had an eating disorder, especially in L.A. The three most common problems I have treated are anorexia, bulimia, and obesity. Some of the eating disorder problems actually come close to rekindling some of my own problems with my weight. As a child I always thought I was overweight and I even remember going on many diets. The following line from one of the diet books always seems to stick in my head: "To you these secrets I divulge in winning the battle of the bulge."

Many patients who binge eat can benefit from a technique where they are exposed to their favorite food and learn to eat only small amounts. I used to give patients an assignment to bring their favorite food into the session. They would then take a small bite of the food at the beginning of the session and resist eating any more for the rest of the session. At the end of this time patients always wanted to just leave the food with me. Confession number 167: There have been many times a patient left a food I really liked and I ended up eating the rest of it during the day. Many other times I would give a patient a suggestion that I would never follow myself. "Mr. O Beese, I think it is important that, if you can't resist eating that food in your house, you throw it out." As long as there are still Jewish mothers alive and millions of people starving to death in the world, there is no way I can waste food.

My biases about food and dieting are clearly evident in working with these patients. I emphasize increasing exercise over reducing food intake, because that is what I do if I need to lose weight. I emphasize eating a little of the "bad" foods rather than complete abstinence, because that is what I do. In the end, I believe most dieting boils down to motivation to lose weight. Most people know how to lose weight and generally know what foods to eat and what to avoid. However, the positive reinforcement value of food is sometimes overwhelming. It is immediate gratification that many people just cannot resist.

August 7

I had to make a house call today. One of the anxiety disorders that I treat is agoraphobia. Some patients with this problem are afraid to leave their house because they think they may have a panic attack. The patient today is someone who called me to do an evaluation of the severity of her problem. She told me that she had been housebound for twenty-six years. She had been forced to leave her house for medical treatment three times during that period. Each time she had to be taken away by ambulance. All of her friends visited her frequently and her sons brought her groceries and anything else she needed.

During my visit I tried to get her to walk past the end of her front walk but she refused. After a short time I realized that this woman was very happy with her problem and really didn't want to get better. She just wanted a mental health professional to verify her disability.

She then could continue to receive money for remaining "sick." In my business we call this secondary gain. I think some people refer to it as criminal behavior.

Some agoraphobics do get better. Another common symptom is that they feel more anxious the farther away they are from their home. I remember working with one patient to help her become comfortable driving away from her home. Every time she went three or four blocks she would start to panic. One day I decided to blindfold her during the ride. After about five minutes she told me that she was very anxious. I told her to take off the blindfold. She discovered that she was in front of the house. I had driven around in circles for the five minutes. It was an effective demonstration of the power of the mind to create panic. However, I am not sure the patient was happy that I deceived her. Confession number 168: If I were a psychiatrist I would have an overwhelming urge to frequently prescribe placebos and see how many of my patients got better.

August 8

Confession number 169: I hate to fail. I have been working with TH for a long time on her fear of elevators. I tried teaching her relaxation skills and then gradually getting on different elevators. I tried flooding by taking her to the highest elevators in L.A. I tried teaching her to change her irrational thoughts about elevators. I even tried a reward and punishment program. I have used every technique known to be effective in treating her and none has worked. I would like to look at this result as her problem, but I can't help taking some responsibility. Today we decided together that there would be one final attempt to treat her. I would admit her to an intensive treatment program where she would get three to four hours of supervised behavioral therapy five days per week for the next three weeks. I would venture to guess that this is the most intensive and costly treatment for elevator phobia ever. I told the patient that I expected her to be significantly improved by the time I got back from my vacation. She asked me how long I was going to be away for and I told her about two years. I am glad she has a sense of humor.

Most of the time I never find out whether a patient who failed in getting better while working with me, has gone on to find help with another therapist. I can't remember any patient calling me to "rub it in." "Hey, Dr. Tarlow this is Jeff Failure. I just wanted to let you know that after you couldn't help me I decided to go see Dr. Miracle. I worked with him for two weeks and I am completely free of my fears."

I believe that an important trait a therapist should posses is the ability to know when he is not helping a patient and to suggest that the patient try another therapist and/or a different type of therapy. The therapist needs to be diplomatic in presenting this to the patient. Some therapists just don't have tact. "I am sorry, Mr. U.R. Toast, I give up. I don't think I can help you. I have given your time to a better patient."

I leave tomorrow for another vacation. Many therapists take their vacation in August. Some even take the entire month of August off. This is a tradition passed down from the psychoanalysts. Given the economics of supply and demand, I sometimes wonder if I should just stay home in August and raise my rates during that month.

August 9 through August 16

Although I remain a staunch behavior therapist and an individual who fully believes in the scientific method, I am beginning to believe more and more in the concept of karma. I must have discussed the concept of binge eating with about four or five different patients the two weeks prior to my vacation. I gave patients tips on how to avoid binge eating. And then the god of karma punished me. He sent me on a cruise! As one passenger described it, a cruise ship has only one meal a day. Unfortunately, it lasts for twenty-four hours. Confession number 170: Every trick I told my patients, I find useless in the face of these temptations. After a few days I believed the chocolate chip cookies were calling my name. Everywhere on the ship I could hear them beckoning me. After the fourth day I was ready to join BEA (binge eaters anonymous) and admit that I was powerless over my ability to resist certain foods. As I eat the final cookie in the airport boarding area, I resolve to start a new diet tomorrow, and it is not even January 1st.

I am pleased that I did not have to work on any patient issues during this vacation. I didn't run into anyone seeking my advice on the plane or on the cruise. However, I was struck by the percentage of overweight people I encountered on the cruise. It is such a prevalent problem. I am sure no one in the buffet line would have appreciated my giving him or her some references for weight control. My favorite weight control book is also my favorite book title: Richard Stuart's *Slim Chance in a Fat World*. It is another one of those problems where people actually don't need a psychologist. Most people know how to lose weight; they just don't have the motivation to follow through.

August 18

Three of my scheduled patients did not show up today. They did not call to cancel. They just didn't show up. I also returned calls from ten new possible patients. Very few of these people actually called me back. Some of them told me they had already made an appointment with another therapist. These problems tend to reinforce my suspicion that being away on vacation is a dangerous thing for a psychologist.

I had a new patient today that brought out an interesting reaction from me. She wore a ring in her bottom lip and I had a great deal of difficulty in making eye contact with her. Every time I would raise my head to look her in the eyes, I would spot the ring and instantaneously get a negative physical reaction. I was extremely happy that the patient did not describe the piercing process to me. However, I can imagine other things that would create an even stronger physical reaction for me. Confession number 171: If I ever have a patient describe to me any type of penile surgery, I believe I would instantly run out of the room holding my testicles.

A representative from the fire department called today to ask me if I knew of a diversion program for hoarders. A diversion program is a therapeutic program that would be a court ordered alternative to jail or prison. For example, some alcohol or drug addicts who commit crimes are put in diversion programs. Similarly, some people who are found guilty of certain assault charges are put into an anger management diversion program. There is no such program for hoarders. However, it led me to think that maybe there should be diversion programs for other problems. How about a diversion program for shoplifters? The name of the facility could be the Neiman Marcus Center for Honest Shopping. Perhaps a diversion program for compulsive gamblers? It could be called Don't Bet on It.

The fire department representative informed me that he had over 900 "clients" who were hoarders. It was his job to make sure their homes were not fire hazards. If they became fire hazards the fire department would come and clean them out. He also told me that in six months the person will have completely replaced all of the hoarded items that were discarded and they would have to clean out the home again. This sounds somewhat similar to living with a teenage son.

August 19

A number of my patients are finishing, cutting back, or quitting therapy. It is mandatory that I make sure the rest of my patients feel good about therapy. Therefore, today I need to reinforce every positive thing my patients have done. Confession number 172: Every time I reinforced a patient I kept thinking of this old song by the Miracles, "I'm Just a Love Machine." Today, I 'm just a reinforcement machine. I try very hard to reinforce every positive thing my patients have done the past few weeks. "That's great, Mr. N. D. Sijon, you finally decided on what car to buy." "Keep up the good work in meeting new people, Ms. D. Pression." "It's great that you only washed your hands four times a day, Mr. Clean." I do all of this reinforcement with a smile on my face.

One of my patients today told me about a very strange dream she was having. As she was walking around the city every person she saw had a face consisting of a doughnut. No eyes, no ears, no mouth, just a doughnut. I decided to ask one of my psychoanalytic friends what they thought this dream might symbolize. I was told that perhaps the doughnut was a symbol for a vagina. I neglected to tell my psychoanalytic friend that just last week she had started a new job in a Krispy Kreme shop.

I spent some time today over at the UCLA program and discovered that TH had quit the intensive program dealing with her fears of elevators. I feel somewhat vindicated in knowing that it probably was not my treatment techniques that resulted in my failing with this patient. There really are times that patients are not motivated to get better. Some patients have managed to rearrange their entire lives to avoid facing their problems. I have heard many therapists say they would like to just grab their patients and shake them. I guess the saying should be: You can lead a patient to the therapist's office, but you can't make him think.

August 21

I received a great deal of reinforcement today from my patients. I had a patient who did not show up for his appointment on time last week and I called him after he was about fifteen minutes late. After realizing he had made a mistake and forgotten about the appointment, I asked him if he would just like to talk on the phone for the remainder of the session. We finished the session on the phone and he said he would mail me a check. Not only did he mail me the check but also he was very grateful that I had called him and allowed him the opportunity to talk on the phone. In the same situation many patients try to talk their way out of paying for the session.

Another patient sent me a note thanking me for my continued patience in treating him. I would say these types of notes come once or twice a year so it is important for me to cherish them. I also received a call today from an ex-patient who told me that he was doing great and that the reason he was so successful was because of me. I didn't argue with him.

A new patient, who was referred by an ex-patient, told me about all of the wonderful things the ex-patient had said about my treatment. I was thinking of using the ex-patient to return calls from all new potential patients. I imagine her telling these new patients the following: "Hello, Ms. D.S. Order, this is Dr. Tarlow's assistant I.M.Cured. I was wondering if you would like to schedule an appointment with the greatest therapist in the world." Sometimes I wonder how I can be the same therapist who is loved by some patients and hated by others.

I had a very attractive new female patient today. At the end of the session she wanted to know if I would possibly consider seeing her for a reduced fee. Confession number 173: Reduced fee, hell, I would treat her for free if she would make her appointments in the middle of the day so that I would not fall asleep.

August 22

It's about that time to update you again on what's happening with some of my patients.

DC is a patient I have seen a few times for treatment of his depression. He shows up ten to fifteen minutes late each session. He is one of several of my patients who are using a workbook in conjunction with my treatment. He is very compliant about doing the homework in the workbook and tends to ask good questions about the reading. I just hope that he doesn't realize that he probably could follow the workbook and save himself a lot of money.

FG continues to be depressed. I have not achieved my goal of getting her to smile in a session. She tested me on movie trivia today and I failed miserably. Maybe I can suggest we watch comedy movies together in the session. Then I can see if Robin Williams can make her smile during the session.

LR is doing better with her OCD assignments. She has tried to get rid of a great deal of clutter in her house and has made significant progress. One thing I have realized with hoarders is that the smaller the house, the worse the problem. LR has about 2,000 videotapes that she has hoarded. If she lived in a 10,000 square foot house and had a room devoted to her videotapes we would call her an avid collector, not a hoarder.

GL's mood is much improved. He has been socializing, exercising, and more productive in his work. The problem is that next week he could be completely depressed. It is my job to try to help him stabilize his mood, something his medications have been unable to do.

Confession number 174: My competitive nature arises again. I would love to have a scoreboard over medications: Tarlow 1 – Zoloft 0.

CK has regressed on his OCD driving assignments. He has not driven in the two weeks since I last saw him. I think sometimes I sound like a nagging mother. "CK, you know the only way you will get better is to practice at least three times per week. And also remember to never go outside in the rain without an umbrella."

NL is my final patient of the day and I continue to talk to her about binge eating strategies. We try an exposure during the session by purchasing four cookies from the restaurant downstairs. She is instructed to take one bite and leave the cookies sitting next to her on the couch for the entire session. The cookies constantly interrupt the session by calling out my name. At the end of the session I ask her to throw the cookies away, preferably in Ohio so that I won't have access to them.

August 25

Today I had a new patient that was a psychologist. In his practice he uses traditional and psychoanalytic therapy techniques. Isn't it interesting that when he needs therapy he comes to a cognitive-behavior therapist and not an analyst? I have often thought about who I would see in L.A. if I needed therapy. Los Angeles Magazine publishes a "Best of L.A." issue every year. They often include lawyers, plumbers, gardeners, masseuses, and other assorted professions. I have never seen any list of the best psychologists in L.A. My first problem in finding a therapist for myself is that I know most of the good cognitive-behavioral therapists in L.A. and it would be considered a "dual relationship" according to ethics committees if I saw any of these people for therapy. If I didn't see a cognitive-behavioral therapist I would be saying to the world: "If you have a problem go to a cognitive-behavioral therapist. However, my problems are different."

One of my patients today was very pessimistic about the fact that she had OCD and would never achieve her goals in life. I often try to use examples in therapy that people can relate to. I was searching for an example of a person who overcame adversity to become successful and decided to talk about Lance Armstrong. To my surprise this strategy backfired when she told me she had never heard of Lance Armstrong. I wanted to ask her what planet she had been living on for the past six years.

Another patient said he was just given a copy of "the article." My OCD interview just won't go away. I am thinking of posting the article in the waiting room with a heading that I am not the Gerald Tarlow, Ph.D. quoted in the article. On a brighter note he told me that his OCD is much better and he thinks that his brain has been somewhat rewired. Confession number 175: I thought I might redo my practice brochure. "Dr. Gerald Tarlow can help you overcome your fears, reduce your anxiety and rewire your brain. Fees include all labor charges, parts extra."

August 26

It is often easy to determine the approximate age of a potential new patient over the phone. If I suspect that someone is older than sixty-five I will ask her about her insurance in order to help me determine if she has Medicare. There are times when I do make a mistake and I am surprised when I open the door to the waiting room. Today I had one of those surprises. One of my new patients was an eighty-seven year-old man. Older people tend to move slower than younger ones. I gave this patient the four or five new patient forms to fill out. Fifteen minutes later he was still working on the first page. Also, before starting the session he needed to go to the bathroom. By the time he returned from the bathroom we had only fifteen minutes left for the first session.

I generally do not see "older" adults in therapy. There are several reasons for this. First, there is a financial reason. Every patient over sixty-five has Medicare health insurance. Medicare has determined the individual psychotherapy with a psychologist is currently worth $103.83. This is the Medicare approved amount. If I am a Medicare provider I am not allowed to charge the patient one-cent more than the Medicare-approved amount. Medicare generally pays fifty percent of the approved amount and the patient is expected to pay the balance if he does not have secondary insurance. Medicare regulations also state that I am not allowed to collect the co-payment until Medicare has paid its share. So, if I see a Medicare patient today I need to have a billing service bill Medicare and then eventually bill the patient for the balance once Medicare pays its share. It is therefore likely that it will take sixty days to get paid for today's session. I often wondered how Medicare came up with $103.83. How does any insurance company figure out the "usual and customary" rate for psychotherapy? I can picture a group of statisticians in Washington sitting around their calculators. "Hey Joe, I know someone who was charged eighty dollars for his therapy. That's nothing Bill. The psychologist who wrote that book *Confessions of a Shrink* I hear charges $220 a session. How about we ask people what they would pay and then add in eighty-three cents. Great idea, Joe, I'll go down to the cafeteria and take a survey."

The other interesting thing about Medicare payments is that the amount that they pay varies depending on the location of your practice in California. I would actually get more money per session if my office was located in a rural area that is underserved by mental health professionals. That has not provided me enough incentive to move my practice to Barstow.

In psychoanalytic terms I also tend to have strong transference reactions to older patients. It is hard for me to not think that I am talking to my mother or father. Confession number 176: There are times when I see these older patients that I never dare slouch in my chair for fear the person will yell at me to sit up straight. It is a stereotype, but many older patients also are very rigid in their thinking. All of my usually persuasive reasoning and logic tends to be lost on many of these patients.

Another stereotype with older patients is hearing problems. Many older patients have actual hearing loss and others seem to hear very selectively. When either of these problems occurs I often feel as if I am dealing with my teenage son. Therefore, I have to repeat myself or yell, both of which I try to avoid until I get home at night.

August 28

Many patients are much better educated about their problems these days than twenty years ago. When I asked a new patient today what her major problem was, she told me that she had "genetic anxiety." I can't seem to find genetic anxiety in the diagnostic manual I use. More and more people are using genetics to explain the reason they have their problems. "Well, Dr. Tarlow, my father had panic attacks and my mother had OCD so that is why I am afraid of driving on the freeway." Other patients come into therapy and tell me that they have a "chemical imbalance." Some patients have even told me that they just need more serotonin. Generally, I don't question their understanding of their disorder. It generally does not matter to me if the anxiety is a learned behavior or you just inherited it from forty-two of your relatives. I will probably treat the problem the same way.

The psychiatrist Lewis Baxter, M.D. did one of my all-time favorite research studies. Dr. Baxter scanned the brains of patients with and without OCD and found that OCD patients had activity in certain areas of the brain that was not present in the people without OCD. He then showed that changes in brain activity could occur if you gave people medications or if they received behavior therapy without medications. When this study came out I felt like all of the work that I had been doing for over thirty years was vindicated. There was now scientific proof that behavior therapy was as effective as medications. Confession number 177: When I first saw the study I wanted to show a copy to my father and say, "You see, Dad, I am a real doctor!"

I came up with a new analogy today in dealing with a phobic patient's fear. I told him that if you saw an insect flying around the room and thought it was a fly that you would probably not be scared. If you identified that same flying insect as a bee, you might start to get scared. I was trying to demonstrate to him the principles of cognitive therapy: it is your interpretation of the situation that makes you anxious, not the situation itself. Unfortunately, this analogy backfired when the patient told me he would also be afraid of flies.

August 29

Today I had an opportunity to watch the television show *Monk*. In this show the lead character, Adrian Monk, is a detective with OCD. They tend to exaggerate many of his OCD symptoms but many of his behaviors are typical of OCD patients. Confession number 178: I was wondering whether more TV shows would start incorporating psychiatric disorders into their main characters. How about *Friends 2*, the story of four "crazy" people living on the streets of New York. Or maybe *The New FBI* starring a paranoid schizophrenic patient. The theme of the show could be "just because he is paranoid doesn't mean that there aren't people out to get him." I could also see a kid's comedy show featuring a ten year-old with ADHD. Just imagine all the silly things that could happen to him because of his psychiatric disorder. See James not paying attention in school. See James be asked the same question three times without answering. See his parents climb the wall!

I think *Monk* took advantage of the success of the movie *As Good As it Gets*. In the movie Jack Nicholson plays a character with OCD. The producers of the movie went to great lengths to portray Nicholson's character correctly. They even consulted with a few of the people at the UCLA OCD Program. The film was critically acclaimed and won many awards. It also probably helped to get many OCD patients into treatment. There are many movies and TV shows that do make mistakes in displaying psychiatric problems. I think I react to these poor portrayals similar to the way sports fans react when they see someone make a stupid play during the game. "Oh crap! I can't believe that he just threw that ball away. That is so stupid!" As for me, I look at the TV and shout, "Oh crap! I can't believe they called that person schizophrenic. When are they ever going to learn that dissociative identity disorder is not schizophrenia?"

Many of my OCD patients are "checkers." Some patients check to see if they have lost something. Typically this involves checking to make sure their wallet and keys are still in their pockets after they get up from a chair. I had a patient today who checked her laundry compulsively. This started to occur after she found that several times she had done her laundry and ended up missing a sock when she went to put the laundry away. Now this is a very tricky problem because I actually believe that this has happened to just about everyone. Where do those socks go? Mostly they seem to be eaten by the clothes dryer. I wanted to put a picture of one of my missing socks on the side of a milk carton with the following caption: "Has anyone seen this sock? It was last seen in the laundry room of Dr. Gerald Tarlow. It is only two years old. Please call 1-800 LOSTSOCKS if you have any information." I imagine that when I die I will see that special place where all of these single socks have gone. That makes it difficult for me to give the patient an assignment to not check the laundry given this international crisis in lost socks.

CHAPTER 12
September

September 1

Today is Labor Day. I decided not to go anywhere this weekend, but no patients want to come in today. I have had a great deal of free time this weekend and have been reading psychology articles that I have hoarded for just such an occasion. Confession Number 179: If I were treating myself for hoarding I probably would have instructed myself to throw these articles out about a year ago.

I would like to share with you some of the articles I was able to complete this weekend. The first article I read was "Brief Cognitive Therapy for Social Phobia." An interesting article, but I am not sure I want to start implementing any techniques that will get people better in only five sessions.

The next article was "Distinguishing Obsessive Features and Worries: The Role of Thought-Action Fusion." This must be a very good article because of the length of the title. It turns out to be very theoretical. Another name for theoretical is boring.

I decided to read an article about medications to see what's new in the psychiatrist's world. "Pharmacologic Treatment of Body Dysmorphic Disorder: Review of Evidence and a Recommended Treatment Approach" is well written and can even be understood by a psychologist! I still hate the fact that all the medications have two names. I have difficulty enough remembering one name.

"Psychotherapy Versus Medication for Depression: Challenging the Conventional Wisdom with Data" is the type of article I like to read to boost my confidence in psychotherapy. By the way, why do most of these articles contain colons in their titles?

Finally, I read "Improving Homework Compliance in the Treatment of Generalized Anxiety Disorder." I was searching for new ways to get people to do their assignments. Unfortunately, I learned I had already known all of these techniques. I will continue to search.

September 2

This turned out to be a very strange day. It started with the dreaded two a.m. page. My pager indicated that someone left an emergency message on my pager voice mail. Half asleep, I called back to find out it was a fax tone. After spending ten minutes calming down the fax tone, I was able to get back to sleep.

My first patient was scheduled for ten a.m. As I opened the door to let her into the session, I saw another patient of mine in the waiting room. It turns out that the other patient was a bit early for her appointment: one week and one hour early. This occurred even though I had phoned this patient a few days ago to confirm her appointment date and time. Confession number 180: I thought maybe she was going to camp out in my waiting room in order to get a better appointment. I think psychotherapy must be in demand, similar to concert tickets. Maybe I will have to start giving out numbers in my waiting room.

My next patient doesn't show up at all. The noon patient shows up twenty minutes early and then another patient shows up at the right time, but three days early. These problems occur even though every one of the patients was given an appointment card. There are times I wish I had made copies of the appointment cards to show the patient that he or she did indeed have an appointment. By the way, all of this is happening without a full moon.

Some patients would make very good therapists. One woman today asked me if I was getting frustrated with her. Of course I denied it, but she was absolutely correct in identifying my feeling. I do tend to get frustrated when I have to repeat myself. If I repeat myself for the eighty-seventh time, my frustration level tends to reach a critical level. I do think there are times I am in need of my own services. If a person who represents himself in a court of law is said to have a fool for a client, I wonder what that would make me if I were my own patient.

September 4

I had an epiphany today while reading the sports page. The name of a pitcher for the Minnesota Twins is Grant Balfour. Now Balfour is probably not the most positive name for a baseball pitcher, but it does seem to be related to his chosen occupation. I remembered that some people's names are closely tied to their professions. In L.A. there is an orthopedic surgeon whose name is Dr. Braiker. There is a therapist who specializes in treating skin pickers whose name is Dr. Pickett. There is also a cardiologist whose name is Dr. Hart. There is a psychologist in L.A. whose name is Ronald Doctor. That's right; his patients call him Dr. Doctor. Confession number 181: If I changed my professional name it might provide me some good free public relations. Additionally, after this book comes out I may be forced to change my name. I have come up with a few possibilities. Dr. Gerald Curethemall seems to generate a lot of positive feelings about going into therapy. If a patient asked if that was my real name I would probably just tell them that my father shortened the name. It used to be Curethemallsky. I think Dr. Feelgood is taken, so I would have to be Dr. Gerald Feelgreat. Great is better than good. Dr. Gerald Shrink would probably offer some confusion to conversations about me. "Hey John, I've got an appointment with my therapist today." "Oh, yeah, what's his name?" "Shrink." "Yeah, your shrink. What's his name?" "Shrink." "Yes, what's his name…?"

It seems like there are so many times when patients bring up issues that are also occurring in my own life. It is likely that I am just paying more attention to when this happens. Since I have been struggling to rehabilitate my knee, I notice that many of my patients are talking about their knee injuries. If my car is being repaired it seems like most of my patients cars are in the shop. If I am arguing with my teenage son, it seems like everyone is arguing with his or her teenage son. I often listen closely to patients talking about these issues in hopes of finding new solutions for my problems. There is no doubt in my mind that if a patient told me about this great treatment for knee pain, I would probably go out and try it.

September 5

Sometimes I am not the only one to use analogies in a session. Today one of my patients told me that her hope was in the toilet. I promised her that I would not flush the toilet. She also started to talk in psychobabble. Psychobabble is an interesting language created by therapists and patients. It consists of many words and phrases that often are meaningless unless you have been in therapy. For example, this patient told me that she was tuning in to her inner critic. However, she also told me that her inner critic was out of tune. No one outside of therapy talks about his or her inner critic. Can you be arrested for killing your inner critic? What if you are critical of your inner critic? Is that your outer critic criticizing your inner critic? Similar to the inner critic is the inner child. I often wondered if I screamed at my inner child if I would be committing inner child abuse.

Freud probably started some of this psychobabble. He used the word "id" to represent the part of the psyche that was the source of instinctual drives. It seems that everywhere I go I run into psychobabble. As I look on my cell phone today I notice that the caller ID indicates that the incoming call is coming from someone with a restricted "id." I wonder how the phone company can know about this caller's unconscious mind.

One of my patients today wants to talk about how she can communicate more effectively with her father. Confession number 182: I must be an expert on this because when my father was alive I knew of every possible way to communicate ineffectively with him. I also find it interesting that teenage patients ask for my advice, and I probably would be the last person on earth that my teenage son would go to for advice. Maybe if I start charging my son for advice he would value it more.

September 6

I am eating a relaxing lunch in a restaurant and I happen to observe someone eating his French fries in a very obsessive compulsive manner. He eats one fry at a time, then straightens his plate with both hands and then eats another fry. Confession number 183: I think they should have a good samaritan law for psychologists. I want to race over to this person and say, "Don't panic, I can help you, I am a psychologist." I actually don't think I would be sued for this type of behavior. However, I think I might be in danger of getting punched in the face.

September 8

Yes, there are some things patients do that are very annoying. Today, you know, I had, you know, a patient say "you know" 137 times in the course of his session, you know. At first I debated whether it was part of my job to tell him how annoying this verbal behavior was. After deciding not to tell him, I did what any self respecting competitive person would do, I counted all of his "you knows" to see if he could set some sort of world record.

I found another topic today where it was difficult for me to be objective. One patient today started to talk about his dissatisfaction with his child's elementary school. It happened to be the same school that I had a problem with when my son was very young. It seems many of the problems I had encountered were still present at this school. I have this overwhelming urge to just give this patient advice and tell him to get his kid out of the school. I sometimes imagine that I will someday have to join AGA (advice givers anonymous). At a group meeting I would get up and say, "Hi, my name is Dr. Tarlow. It's been three months since I've given a patient advice."

I received a message today from a patient's wife. I had seen this patient one time about five months ago. Part of her message said that I had diagnosed her husband with severe COD. This seemed amazing to me because I really do have trouble differentiating halibut from cod. I also was not aware that I could diagnose a person as having a fish. Maybe I misunderstood. Maybe I had diagnosed her husband with some form of mail delivery disorder. Later in the day one of my colleagues was kind enough to tell me that he thought the patient's wife had it backwards and that she really meant to say OCD. Confession number 184: In order for this problem to never happen again I made a list of some of the possible disorders that a dyslexic person might talk to me about. A child might be suffering from DDA. Someone having experienced a severe trauma could have developed DSTP. If you worry excessively about your appearance you may have DDB. I probably could reassure these people by telling them that I have a D.hP. in clinical psychology.

September 9

When I was a kid I used to collect baseball cards. It now seems that there are cards for just about every sport. I have also seen cards for entertainers and musicians. However, I have not seen psychology trading cards. I could see a group of psychologists sitting around a convention trying to trade cards. "Hey, Doc, I'll give you a B.F. Skinner for your Freud. No way, Jose, how about you throw in a Dr. Phil." They could even have rookie cards for newly licensed therapists. On a similar note, they could also make cards of the different psychological disorders. For example, you could trade major depression for anorexia.

One of my patients today told me that he thought his head was going to explode. I tried to reassure him that heads couldn't actually explode while moving my chair farther away from him.

I saw six patients today and didn't feel particularly good about my work. I just seemed a little "off" in my comments and questions. Confession number 185: I hope that I am not going into a slump. Psychologists must have slumps just like every other profession. There is a new offshoot of psychotherapy called "coaching." If I am in a slump, maybe it would be good for me to hire a coach. If I hire a coach I probably should also have some cheerleaders. I think I'll start interviewing for the cheerleaders first. I picture some very attractive young females in short skirts and pompoms leading cheers in my waiting room. "Tarlow, Tarlow he's our man. If he can't cure them no one can!"

September 11

Psychologists have dreams too. I dreamed last night that I was doing an initial interview with a patient. The patient was a psychologist. At the end of the session I tried to schedule another appointment with this new patient. I told him that I had an opening next Monday at eleven. As it turns out I really did have an opening next Monday at eleven. He said he could not make that time and I told him the only other opening I had was in Calabasas on Thursday. Remarkably, that was also the only day of the week he was in Calabasas. At that point my alarm clock went off which allowed me to end this session with this very nice male psychologist. I strongly suspect that I was both the therapist and the patient in this dream. I therefore did not charge this patient for the session.

I received a call today from my local phone company to see if I was interested in renewing my ad in the yellow pages. The only ad I have ever paid for was just a simple listing of my name in the yellow pages. Many psychologists do choose to place a large ad in the yellow pages. I assume the hope is that people pick their psychologist in the same manner they pick their drain cleaning service. I decided to look at some of the ads in the yellow pages to determine if I should place a big ad this year.

The first thing I notice when I am searching for the psychologist listings is that they come right after the listings for psychics in the phone book. I hope that some patients do not make a careless mistake and phone their local psychic instead of a psychologist. The psychics do seem to have prettier ads. There are about ten big ads in the psychologist section. The ads try to incorporate some catchy phrases like, "We can work it out." Or, "Have someone listen to you for a change." How about "Maximize your potential; achieve your goals." Confession number 186: I figure if I were to place an ad I would need a better catch phrase. I have tried to adapt some of the phrases from the plumbing section of the phone book. I certainly like "and away go troubles down the drain." Or, "Head stopped up? Call the pros." I am sure that "fast, friendly service" is also what a lot of patients are looking for. However, there are a few phrases I will probably have to leave out. "Lifetime guarantee" is not advisable in my business. I think the twenty-four-hour; seven-day service is also something that I won't offer. In the end I decide that I am still not going to place a big ad in the yellow pages.

September 12

Dr. Phil was on television tonight in a special about obesity. He was hawking his "revolutionary" book on how to lose weight. Note to Dr. Phil: there is nothing revolutionary about your approach to losing weight. Richard Stuart wrote a book about thirty years ago titled *Slim Chance in a Fat World* that covered just about all of your revolutionary weight loss principles. Why do psychologists write books? This is the fourth book I have written so I have a pretty good idea of some of the reasons. Many academic psychologists write textbooks to try to sell them to students. I do believe that a good introductory psychology text can make you rich. Unfortunately, some areas of psychology, such as physiological psychology, attract far fewer students. I believe that most of the academicians who write books for these areas are truly trying to improve the quality of the education experience for the students.

Some psychologists like Dr. Phil write self-help books. The idea is generally to choose a problem that is so pervasive that if one per cent of the people with that problem buy the book you will become rich. Obesity, relationships and addictions top the list. Some psychologists figure they have seen so many patients with a particular disorder that they might as well just write about the disorder.

There is also a generally accepted rule that states if your first self-help book is a success, that you write a sequel essentially saying the same thing. That is why we not only have the hit book *Men are From Mars and Woman are From Venus*, but we also have *Mars and Venus in the Bedroom*, *Mars and Venus on a Date*, and *The Mars and Venus Diet and Exercise Solution*. I am anxiously awaiting *Mars and Venus Do the Dishes*, *Mars and Venus at the Mall*, and *Mars and Venus in the Bathroom*. Writing this book has forced me to think of all of the sequels I will have to write. Confession number 187: So far I have come up with *Confessions of a Frustrated Jock*, *Confessions of a Junk Food Junkie*, and *Confessions of a Red Sox Fan*.

September 15

I bumped into another psychologist today who I had known for many years. He told me that he was retiring at the end of next week after being in practice for twenty-eight years. This made me think of what it would be like to retire and some of the important things that would need to be done when a psychologist retires. For example, I asked my friend what message he was going to put on his answering machine after he retires. He told me that he would tell people that he is no longer in practice and give instructions for getting in touch with him. Confession number 188: I think my message would say; "This is Dr. Tarlow. I'm unable to take your call right now, or tomorrow, or the next day, or for that matter for the rest of my life."

He also told me that he was terminating therapy with one patient that he had seen for twenty-eight years. I assume that the timing was perfect and that the patient was due to finish therapy in twenty-eight years. By the way, twenty-eight years of therapy at $150 a session adds up to over $200,000. I guess I should start preparing some of my patients for my retirement in four years.

What does one do with twenty-eight years of patient records? The lawyers tell us not to throw these away. I guess after I retire I could have a room in my house devoted just for patient records. If anyone asked what was in the room I would just tell him it was my record collection.

I know that I would take my pager off and throw it as far as I could into the ocean. I would hope that it didn't hit one of my patients who I encouraged to swim for exercise.

I definitely would want a going-out-of business sale, a sort of professional garage sale. Anyone want thirty years of a Behavior Therapy journal? How about a great selection of used psychological test equipment? I'm sure someone could use a few thousand sheets of Center for Anxiety Management stationery.

When people begin a practice they sometimes send out announcements. Why not a going out of business announcement? "Dr. Gerald Tarlow is proud to announce that he is no longer seeing patients. He will no longer be seeing patients in West L.A. or in Calabasas. If you need to talk to him for any reason, too bad."

September 16

Another day, another brand new phobia. A new patient today told me that he was afraid of eating breakfast in his breakfast room. I tried to guess the origin of this phobia but failed miserably. I thought that perhaps he had become sick when eating in the breakfast room. I thought he might have gotten into too many arguments with his wife in the breakfast room. Perhaps he choked on some food in the breakfast room. None of these hypotheses were correct. The reason he feared eating breakfast in his breakfast room was that one day when he was eating breakfast a car crashed through the outside wall of his breakfast room and stopped a few feet away from him. When the room was finally rebuilt he became anxious every time he sat down to eat in the room. I told him that this of course was a common phobia that I have treated many times before. I told him that I get most of my referrals from the construction companies that rebuild people's houses after similar accidents.

One of the principles of cognitive therapy that I use with people is to point out the difference between probability and possibility. I like people to believe that just because anything is possible does not mean that it is highly probable that it will occur. For example, it is possible that a plane you are on will crash, but it is not very probable. It is possible that your house will burn down if you don't check to make sure the gas is off, but it is not very probable. Most patients buy this type of reasoning. However, when the "freak" accidents do occur, patients love to abandon the laws of probability. "Hey, Dr. Calm, I know you said the chances of a plane crashing was one in seven million, but did you see that picture on the front page of the Decrepit Airline crash where all 147 people died?" My usual response to this type of logic is, "Mr. Hysteric, can you tell me the last time you saw a newspaper headline that read: 'Today 40,000 Planes Took Off and Landed Safely?'"

These probability lessons also allow me to use another rule that I learned in statistics. If three things have to happen in order for the dreaded event to occur, the probability of the dreaded event occurring is figured by multiplying together the probability of each of three events occurring. For example, the probability of my house getting robbed because I forgot to lock the door is equal to the probability that I didn't lock the door times the probability a thief was in the neighborhood times the probability that he will rob my house during the time the door is unlocked. So, let's say that there is a one in a hundred chance the patient didn't lock the door and there is a one in a thousand chance that there was a thief in the neighborhood and there was a one in a thousand chance the thief tried my door to see if it was unlocked. The actual odds of my house being robbed would be one in ten million. Hopefully, these odds help the patient to not go back to check his door.

I will try to use these principles with my new patient but, given the fact that a car already crashed through his breakfast room, I will have to try to convince him it is very unlikely that "lightening strikes twice." Confession number 189: I briefly thought that I could cure his problem by just asking him to install a stop sign in front of his breakfast room.

September 18

I have a new panic disorder patient today. As I went to greet him in the waiting room he told me that he is having a panic attack. Even after seeing hundreds of patients with anxiety disorders, it would have been impossible for me to guess that this patient was currently in the middle of a panic attack. This is actually a first for me, a patient having a panic attack in my waiting room before I ever see him. I feel like I am working in an emergency room. I should instantly change into a white lab coat and start working on this patient. After thirty minutes of "instant cure" therapy this patient's panic attack has not stopped. I have taught him how to breathe properly and gave him some of my best guided imagery instructions for relaxation. Nothing worked. My credibility was rapidly shrinking. Confession number 190: I had a strong desire to unwrap one of the Jolly Rancher candies in my desk, hand it to the patient and say: "Suck on this medication for three minutes. It is guaranteed to stop your panic attack."

I had to convince the patient that the reason my techniques did not work was that he had not practiced them sufficiently. I convinced him to make another appointment with me. I intend to be more thoroughly prepared for his next panic attack.

One of my patients wanted my opinion of which NBA players cheat on their wives. I told him that it would take less time to discuss which players probably do not cheat on their wives. After about fifteen minutes we could only come up with Derek Fisher and Mark Madsen.

My last patient of the day spent a great proportion of the session trying to convince me that she was a genius. I kept thinking if she was that smart, she probably didn't need me and could treat herself. I did have a desire to administer an IQ test just for the fun of it.

September 19

Advice columns have appeared in newspapers for many years. Many of the people who write these columns are mental health professionals. There are also other columns, such as Dear Abby that I think are written by Jewish mothers. I recently came across a question in Dear Abby that spiked my interest. "Dear Abby: I have been dating 'Lowell' for more than a year. He's a college graduate with a professional job. We have begun talking marriage, and I am thrilled, but I have one concern: Lowell believes he is from another planet. ... What should I do? Not Easy Being an Earth Girl." I wondered if this was a real question or just someone's idea of a good joke. Confession number 191: I decided I would need to test this question by writing several questions and submitting them to various advice columns around the country. Here are a few of my questions:

Dear Abby,

I have recently been diagnosed as having paranoid schizophrenia. One of my symptoms is that I hear voices. Recently the voices have been telling me to do certain things. For example, the voices told me to jump out of my car. I actually listened to the voices and did this last week. Luckily the car was still parked in the garage. Please help.

Schizophrenic Miss

Dear Dr. Phil,

I have a perplexing relationship problem that I thought you might be able to help me with. Every time my wife and I have sex she howls like a wolf. I now find myself curiously drawn to going to the zoo and looking at wolves. I get very excited when I see them. What should I do?

Animal Lover

I am anxiously awaiting the advice columnists' answers.

September 22

The Emmy awards were on last night and the winner of the best actor in a comedy series was Tony Shalhoub who plays Monk, the obsessive compulsive detective. I guess the voters believe that these obsessive compulsive symptoms are hysterical. I don't think most of my patients would agree.

I think psychology really should have a similar award show. I am sure that millions of television viewers have been in therapy and would be interested in such an award show. The show could have the usual broad categories such as outstanding male therapist, outstanding female therapist, outstanding group therapist, outstanding child therapist and outstanding family therapist. I am sure there could also be some awards reserved for more specific categories such as outstanding cognitive behavior therapist, outstanding gestalt therapist or outstanding psychoanalytic therapist. Then, it may also be possible to honor some subspecialties such as outstanding orthodox Jewish therapist or outstanding gay and lesbian therapist.

Confession number 192: I would look forward to some of the more bizarre categories such as the best therapist to never engage in continuing education. I also think an award for the therapist who has seen the most patients during the year is long overdue. A lifetime achievement award could be given to any therapist who retires without having been sued.

You may be wondering who votes for these awards. I would like to propose a system similar to the baseball all-star balloting.

Every time you attend a therapy session there could be ballots in the therapist's waiting room. You could take as many as you want and send them in.

September 23

One of the therapists in the UCLA OCD program is leaving the program and I am one of the people responsible for hiring a new therapist. The program received about twenty applications for the position. Each applicant submitted his vita summarizing his education and experience. After reviewing the paperwork, I have come to the conclusion that there are certain things one should avoid putting on paper when applying for a psychologist job in a hospital. (1) Experience gained at Taco Bell in high school is not relevant for a psychologist position. (2) Publishing forty-two articles on the effects high sugar consumption in teenage baboons is not helpful. (3) Attending a graduate school located in Aruba and accredited in Zimbabwe is not an advantage. And (4) stating that your ultimate goal is to have a program similar to Dr. Phil's will not advance your application.

After reviewing the paperwork I narrowed down the applicants to four candidates. All of the four people were invited for an interview. Each person possesses a Ph.D. in psychology. Over the past several days I have interviewed all of the candidates.

Confession number 193: Having a Ph.D. in psychology does not mean that you automatically possess common sense. The first candidate told me that if he gets the job he only intends to remain with the program about one year. Maybe if he were completely honest he would have just told me that he would be glad to stay until a better job came along. I told you that I teach my patients to lie. Why didn't someone teach this person to lie? "Dr. Tarlow, this is the job I have been waiting for. I really want to work with you and I can envision being here for at least ten years." This type of lie is so small the candidate probably wouldn't have even had to go to confessional the following Sunday.

The second candidate was better. She answered most of the questions correctly and appeared truly motivated to work with me. Unfortunately, I believe that this candidate actually has about three psychiatric diagnoses. Unlike a job for alcoholism counselor, actually having OCD is not a prerequisite for this job.

The third candidate was actually friendly and had a sense of humor. My type of person.

The fourth candidate was perhaps the best person on paper. I would probably hire this person as soon as she gets a personality. I decided in favor of the friendly person.

September 25

I have a new patient scheduled for this morning. As I entered the lobby of the building that houses my office I noticed a person dressed up as a coffee cup. I started to pray that this is not my new patient. I thought about how I would start the session with him. "Well, Mr. Cup, what seems to be the problem? Had a little too much caffeine today? I bet you can't get a handle on your problems. Do you think that everyone is looking at you?" It could be that this person has a vocational problem. He may be an out of work mascot. Luckily for me he did not follow me up to my office.

My initial patients today were quite pleasant and I feel I have helped them. However, my third patient of the day was a problem. I was seeing this person for a reevaluation for the UCLA OCD program. The patient was already fifteen minutes late so I decided to call his spouse and find out where he was. His wife told me he was on his way and I waited patiently for him. After he did not show up for his appointment I left the office to get some lunch. Guess who I bumped into getting off the elevator? He tells me that he was lost and I tell him that I would be happy to reschedule his appointment. We returned back to my office to reschedule the appointment. When we got back into the office I told the patient that I would be glad to reschedule the appointment but he must pay me for today's session. At this point the patient started to verbally attack me. He told me that I do not care about people; that I am not a psychologist; all I am is a businessman. I made an instantaneous decision that I never want to see this person again. The only way I can do this is to not charge him. I ripped up his check, told him that I am not charging him, and asked him to get out of my office and never come back. I felt good that I was assertive, but the incident put a damper on an otherwise good therapeutic day.

Confession number 194: I try to think of other passive-aggressive ways to get even with this patient. I could schedule another appointment for him, put him in an empty therapy room when he arrives, and leave him there the whole day. I could send him a letter telling him that he was absolutely correct about my being a businessman and therefore I have sent him a bill for the missed session including interest. I could also send him a phony letter from the Better Business Bureau. "Dear Ms. Informed: We are investigating several complaints from patients of Dr. Gerald Tarlow. Numerous people are complaining that Dr. Tarlow actually charges them for therapy. We at the Better Business Bureau want you to know that we will do everything in our power to make sure that he never makes another cent doing therapy. Please help our cause by picketing his office to make sure that no other people are actually charged for his time."

About forty-five minutes after the patient left his wife called me and I explained the situation to her. She said, "Now you know what I have to put up with."

September 26

I had a particularly hard time today getting patients to talk. After I tried the usual "Hello, how are you?" I often go to the "what's happening?" question. Following this I often try "What's been going on since our last session?" None of these questions seemed to be yielding much verbal information from my patients today. Confession number 195: I think about going to auctioneer school to learn to talk very rapidly and continually for the entire session just in case the patients have nothing to say. I have also thought about developing various scripts for patients. This would be similar to psychotherapy karaoke. Patients could choose their problem, e.g. panic disorder, and I would hand them a script that would contain all the responses to my questions. For example, "Hello, Ms. Silent, how are you?" "Dr. Tarlow, I had three panic attacks the past week and I am now afraid to go shopping in the mall." I would make sure that the scripts would not allow the patients to go over their forty-five-minute sessions.

Patients often do not do things in their own best interests. One of my OCD patients told me today that she has to repeat most of her behaviors a certain number of times. She has to repeat them the same number of times as the jersey number of her favorite football player. Unfortunately, her favorite football player wears number ninety-six. I decide to file this information under "help for people who may develop OCD." It is important that when deciding on a favorite sports player that you choose someone whose number is zero, one, or two.

I had a few very interesting conversations with other therapists in my suite today. No, we did not talk about patients or therapy. We talked about vacations, toys we bought, and who is moving into the vacant office next door. We decided that the vacant office is "jinxed." Since we have been in the building, about ten different people have occupied the office and no one has been successful. Psychologists can be superstitious.

September 29

I thought that one final update on some of my patients might be helpful. BK, in her predictable fashion, has cancelled the last two sessions the day before the session. I have a strong urge to just charge her by the year and let her attend as many sessions as she wants. BK will be in therapy for the rest of her life.

FG continues to be depressed and unable to follow most of my therapeutic suggestions. I have decided to try some very simple suggestions. The suggestion for this week is that some people consider it exercise if you get out of bed to urinate at least three times per day. FG will be in therapy for the rest of her life.

TH still has no desire to work on her elevator phobia. However, she always has an important issue to discuss that takes precedence over her phobia. I think the important issue for today was the California election. TH will be in therapy for the rest of her life.

LO is better. His OCD is much improved and he has actually cut back on his therapy sessions with me. Unfortunately, because of all of his family problems, LO will be in therapy with his other therapist for the rest of his life.

MW continues to make small improvements. However, since he has been depressed most of his life, he has never learned some very basic skills such as cooking a meal. Therefore, MW will be in therapy for the rest of his life.

Confession number 196: I imagine that when I retire I will have to tell these patients that they are not done with therapy. "I know you have made significant progress in therapy with me. I really, really believe that if you work hard with your next therapist that you could be finished with therapy in another fifteen or twenty years."

September 30

One year has passed in the life of my practice. In many ways this past year has been very typical of many of my previous years of full time private practice. There have been a few highlights and some disappointments. There were actually very few disappointments the past year. Clinically, there were people I wanted to help and couldn't. There were a few patients who didn't like me and quit therapy. There were a few patients who got angry with me. There were several patients I truly disliked. None of these disappointments were horrible.

There were many patients who told me how grateful they were for my help, but I think the one that stands out the most for me was one of the patients with a fear of flying who I helped overcome her fear. Having her tell me that I had changed her life felt great. It was also important to me that her problem was helped with the virtual reality equipment. I felt good that after all these years of practice I could incorporate a new technique into my therapeutic repertoire.

Another highlight of my year was my promotion at UCLA from associate to full clinical professor. It is probably only status, but whenever I achieve something that few of my colleagues have achieved I feel like I was the winning pitcher in the final game of a world series.

To all my patients who put their trust in me, I thank you for that. I really tried everything I know to help you make changes in your life.

For all the patients who still owe me money, pay up, I deserve to be paid. And one final confession: Confession number 197: I love my work and I love finding humor in anything. I wish that everyone could laugh just a little bit more. Thank you for allowing me to share my innermost thoughts with you.

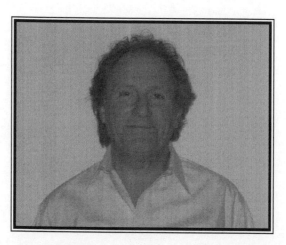

Gerald Tarlow received his Ph.D. in Clinical Psychology from the University of Montana. He is a clinical professor in the Department of Psychiatry at UCLA. He is also the director of the Center For Anxiety Management. He lives in Calabasas, California with his wife and son.